JIM & GLENDA CHATHAM

Increasing the Joy: Studies in 1 John

Studies in 1 John

HAROLD T. BRYSON

BROADMAN PRESS
Nashville, Tennessee

© Copyright 1982 • Broadman Press
All rights reserved.

4213-90

ISBN: 0-8054-1390-1
Dewey Decimal Classification: 227.94
Subject Heading: BIBLE. N.T. 1 JOHN
Library of Congress Catalog Card Number: 81-67200

Printed in the United States of America

Scripture quotations from *The Bible: a New Translation* by James A.R. Moffatt are used by permission. Copyright © 1935 by Harper and Row, Publishers, Inc.

Scripture quotations from *The New English Bible* are reprinted by permission. Copyright © The Delegates of the Oxford University Press, 1961, 1970.

To
Ernest Mosley
and
James C. Barry
two men who recognized a gift and gave me my first opportunity to teach preaching skills to pastors

Preface

My desire to write on 1 John first came to mind when I taught "Preaching from 1 John" during Bible-Preaching Week at Glorieta Conference Center in Glorieta, New Mexico. The plenary sessions resulted in stimulating group discussions and in therapeutic private conversations. My interest in 1 John intensified with involvement in Bible conferences, preaching workshops, and classroom lectures at New Orleans Baptist Theological Seminary. Teaching and preaching from 1 John has helped me focus on many questions which believers ask about Christian living in today's world. Also, my experiences with 1 John have helped me provide a model for preaching or teaching a Bible book and for structuring a particular lecture or sermon.

The predominant theme of this book is that Christians may increase their joy in the Lord. Central to the theme of this work is that the Christian begins a relationship with the Lord by a vital union with him and enhances that relationship by a continuing communion with the Lord. This book contains a brief background of 1 John and thirteen subsequent studies of timely topics based on passages from 1 John. The format may be characterized as studies. Not enough exhortation, illustrations, and application exist in the chapters to call them sermons. These are studies to help pastors, church leaders, and other believers increase the joy of their Christian lives. Most biblical references are taken from the Revised Standard Version of the Bible (copyrighted 1946, 1952, © 1971, 1973). References marked (KJV) are from the King James Version of the Bible.

Personal indebtedness to many individuals and groups must be expressed. That collective group from congregations across America who came to Glorieta in 1979 deserve appreciation. Their interest in the studies and their encouragement motivated me to write this work. Many churches, student groups, and pastors have been kind to listen to these studies. My colleagues at New Orleans Baptist Theological Seminary have provided an environment for creative thinking and for writing. Dr. Billy Simmons, my colleague at the seminary who is professor of New Testament and Greek, has helped me immeasurably with New Testament thought and language. My gratitude also goes to Barbara Bryant for typing initial drafts and to Ruth Ann Kinchen for typing the final copy. Kathryn Harper is to be thanked for putting the manuscript in its initial form.

Finally, I am grateful to Judy, my wife, and to William and Thomas, our two sons. They knew that husband-father was writing, teaching, or preaching in order to help believers increase the joy of Christian living. Numerous hours have been given to the study, pulpit, and lectern with 1 John, time which probably belonged to them.

Contents

1. Getting a Letter from the Lord 13
2. Jesus Christ Is Real (1:1-4) 21
3. Taking Sin Seriously (1:5 to 2:2) 31
4. Becoming Better Believers (2:3-11) 39
5. Spiritual Passages (2:12-14) 49
6. Coping with a World System (2:15-17) 57
7. Will the Real Christian Please Stand? (2:18-27) 65
8. A Letter from the Father (2:28 to 3:3) 75
9. Let Me Show You My Children (3:4-18) 85
10. Getting Help from God (3:19 to 4:6) 95
11. Learning About a Loving God (4:7-12) 105
12. Making Sure You Are a Christian (4:13 to 5:5) 113
13. Hearing from the Witnesses (5:6-12) 123
14. Making Gigantic Affirmations (5:13-21) 131
    Notes 141

Increasing the Joy: Studies in 1 John

1
Getting a Letter from the Lord

Going to the mailbox has to be one of life's most interesting activities. Each visit of the postal carrier brings various possibilities. Of course each month the mail brings notification of car payments, house notes, drug purchases, doctors' bills, and other bills. These notices do not excite us as much as other pieces of mail. Invitations to social or business functions come. Ones we dearly love send us letters. All kinds of letters are delivered by the postal service. The daily delivery builds suspense in each one of us.

Suppose you received a letter from the Lord. Believers *have* been given a letter from the Lord. The First Letter of John belongs to the category of letters even though it does not begin or end like a typical, first-century letter. It has no opening salutation and no closing greetings, such as the letters of Paul and other first-century writings. Yet, one cannot read this document without feeling that it is, indeed, a letter. It has an intensely personal tone, and the writer had a definite situation and a definite group of people in mind. First John belongs to the category of letters because it was not written to the church at large but to congregations of one area in which the author had a longstanding relationship. It was a letter inspired of the Lord to meet an immediate need created by a critical situation.

The Bible is a divine-human book. Each book of the Bible comes to us out of divinely inspired, historical life situations. The Letter of 1 John is one which was divinely inspired and intended to address real situations which prevailed toward the latter part of the first century. The goal of this book is to aid believers' understanding of what God is saying to us today through 1 John. To understand this letter of the Lord, we must discover, as much as possible, what the New Testament writer meant when God first inspired him to write it. Some facts about the letter will help frame God's message to us.

The Author of the Letter

The name of the author does not appear in any chapter of the letter. How then is authorship determined? Usually human authors of biblical books are determined by internal and external evidences. Since there is no specific internal mention of the author, we need to look for external evidences about the author. There are different ideas about the authorship of 1, 2, and 3 John. Some traditions ascribe them to John, the apostle of Jesus. Others ascribe them to a John the elder. There are five books in the New Testament which have been called Johannine. These are the Fourth Gospel, Revelation, 1, 2, and 3 John.

A variety of views have been held by biblical scholars about the relation of these five New Testament writings. Some of these views are as follows:

1. All five books were written by one man.

2. Revelation was written by one man, and the other four were written by another man.

3. Revelation was written by one man, the Gospel and 1 John by a second author, and 2 and 3 John by a third author.

4. Revelation was written by one man, the Gospel by another, and 1, 2, and 3 John were written by a third author.

This study adopts the strong tradition that all five books known as the Johannine literature were written by one man, the apostle John. This conclusion is not without strong grounds of support. First, there are great similarities of subject matter, style, and vocabulary. This can be especially noticed with a close comparison of 1, 2, and 3 John with the Gospel of John. Second, there are strong external evidences that the apostle John was the author. There are allusions to John in the writings of Clement of Rome (AD 96), Polycarp, and Papias (both died AD 150). Irenaeus, who wrote in the middle of the second century, ascribed the work to the "disciple of

Getting a Letter from the Lord

the Lord." Also in the third century, Dionysius and Cyprian attributed 1 John to John the apostle.

John the apostle was the son of Zebedee and Salome. He had a brother named James. His family was engaged in the fishing industry at Capernaum near the Sea of Galilee. Both John and James became disciples of the Lord. John was one of the "inner circle," being present with James and Peter at the raising of Jairus' daughter, the transfiguration, and Jesus' visit to Gethsemane. At the crucifixion, Jesus entrusted his mother to John's care. In the Book of Acts, the records are clear that John worked with Peter in the church at Jerusalem.

According to tradition, John remained in Jerusalem until the death of Mary, the mother of Jesus. Her death was reported to have happened near the middle of the first century. Irenaeus's writings inform us that John took up residence in Ephesus. He preached and ministered in this significant city until his banishment to Patmos near the end of the first century. Many competent New Testament scholars believe that the Gospel and the three letters were all written while John lived in Ephesus. So, the apostle John probably wrote 1 John from Ephesus during the last quarter of the first century.

The Occasion of the Letter

Having discussed briefly who wrote the letter, we need to see why he wrote the letter. Every letter has some reason or reasons behind it. The Letter of 1 John is no exception. Judging from the contents of the letter, we can conclude that John was compelled to write. The apostle's long work in the churches of the Roman province of Asia was in jeopardy. Some church members had seceded from the main body. They set themselves up as a rival Christian church. They claimed to have the only true doctrine and fellowship. They not only attracted followers but also disturbed believers in the church throughout Asia. A careful reading of 1 John will disclose that false prophets prevailed whom John described as "antichrists" (cf. 1 John 2:18,22). Something had to be done. The believers' joy was greatly disturbed. The Lord inspired John to write a letter to the church or churches in Ephesus and the surrounding region.

Perhaps the best identification of the false teachers or "antichrists" comes from Neil Alexander's work *The Epistles of John: Introduction and Commentary*. Using references in 1 John to the false teachers, Alexander diagnosed the problem with the labels of Gnosticism, Docetism, and Cerinthianism.[1] *Gnosticism* was a philosophy which began to develop near the end of the first century. Its basic premises were that spirit is inherently good, and matter is inherently evil. God, according to the Gnostics, was entirely spirit, therefore, wholly good. Gnostics also believed that the spiritual part of a human being was good. Only the good part could know God. The Gnostics claimed that only the material side of human life hindered a relationship with God. Using elaborate rites known only to the Gnostics, they felt that they could transcend their material environment. Through these rites, they claimed to have a union with the Divine Spirit.

We can see from this brief identification of Gnosticism how believers were disturbed and robbed of joy. First, a religious experience was authenticated by the secret rites of the Gnostics. Through these rituals, the false teachers claimed to know or to abide in the Lord. Second, the premise of matter as evil was opposed to the Christian concept of God's creation and of the incarnation. Third, the claim to have a spiritual union with God led to a disdain of the material. The Gnostics, because of their claim of spiritual union with God, felt they were above sin.

Docetism was another word Neil Alexander used to describe the false teachers. Christians spread the gospel throughout Asia. The pagan Gnostics welcomed it, for to them it represented another way of knowing God. The more these Gnostics heard of Christianity the more they said that Christians held on to obsolete myths. One myth they disliked was that Jesus Christ had come in the flesh. They felt that the true God, the Pure Spirit, could not be involved with the evil material world and bodily flesh. So many said that Jesus really did not become a man. He only seemed to be a man, to have a human body. This philosophy was known as Docetism, from the Greek word *dokein* which means "to seem." While professing to be Christians, these false teachers (Docetics) said that the incarnation was not real.

The third word Neil Alexander used to describe the false teachers was *Cerinthianism*. This word comes from *Cerinthus,* a first-century Gnostic, who accepted the human life of Jesus but not his divinity. He separated "Jesus" from "the Christ." Cerinthus claimed that Jesus was born of a sexual union of Mary and Joseph. Divinity descended upon Jesus at his baptism and left just before his crucifixion. Cerinthianism denied the full divinity of Jesus.

With the prevalence of the ideas of Gnosticism, Docetism, and Cerinthianism, John had to write to believers. He was appalled not only by the succession and the heresies but also he was disturbed about the churches of Asia. Many of the believers were uncertain. They gave serious consideration to the beliefs of the false teachers. They were influenced by the ethics of the heretics. The believers' joy of communion with the Lord was greatly disturbed. God inspired John to write a letter so that the believers' joy would be increased. John wanted to recall the fundamental truths of Christianity and to assure the believers of their standing with the Lord.

The Purposes of the Letter

Closely akin to the occasion of the letter are the purposes. John wrote for the good of the believers throughout the Roman province of Asia. The believers were being influenced by the ideas promoted by the false teachers. John's purposes for the letter are not hard to detect. Throughout 1 John, the writer stated his purposes which were generally introduced by the statement, "we are writing this that" (1 John 1:4; see also 2:1,26; 5:13). These statements introduce the purposes of the letter.

There are four purposes which John mentioned for writing his letter. The first purpose was to increase the believers' joy: "We are writing this that our joy may be complete" (1 John 1:4). The idea of joy referred to the idea of fellowship with God and with each other.

Without a doubt, the believers' joy of fellowship with God was hindered by the false teachers. John wrote so that communion with the Lord would be enhanced, which would intensify the believers' joy. I think the comprehensive purpose of 1 John is to increase the believers' joy by telling about union and communion with the Lord as a basis of standing and fellowship with him.

The second purpose of 1 John was to increase the believers' joy by decreasing sin: "My little children, I am writing this to you so that you may not sin" (1 John 2:1). A believer's happiness is disturbed by sin. Therefore, John wrote to the Christians for the purpose of helping them become more like the Master. John wanted them to move more from where they were to where they ought to be.

A third purpose of 1 John was to promote doctrinal accuracy: "I write this to you about those who would deceive you" (1 John 2:26). The believers' joy was disturbed by the diverse ideas about Jesus Christ. Heretics tried to get the church away from its belief about Jesus. John wanted his readers to affirm the humanity of Jesus, as well as his divinity.

A fourth purpose of 1 John was to give assurance to disturbed believers: "I write this to you who believe in the name of the Son of God, that you may know that you have eternal life" (1 John 5:13). The believers could have no joy with uncertainties filling their minds about their experiences with the Lord, about the person of Jesus, and about Christ's commands. John wrote to give confidence or certainty to them.

The general theme of this study of 1 John will be *increasing the joy*. The other purposes will be subordinate to this theme. When believers open themselves more to the Lord, their joy will be increased, their sins will be decreased, their convictions about Jesus Christ will be confirmed, and their uncertainties will be settled.

The Style of the Letter

Two extremes prevail about the style of 1 John. On one hand, some interpreters see no design at all in 1 John. They say that the writer was a contemplative mystic who wrote his thoughts in the form of detached and isolated sayings. On the other hand, some scholars have discerned an order in the letter.

A study of any biblical book will be enhanced if one reads and studies the flow of the writer. The Letter of 1 John begins with an introduction about the reality of Jesus Christ in 1:1-4. In the main body of the letter, one can ascertain three movements of thought. The author gives three characteristics of God and proceeds to show that believers in union and communion with the Lord share the Lord's nature. The three movements are God as light 1:5 to 2:27, God as righteousness 2:28 to 4:6, and God as love 4:7 to 5:12. The letter closes with some affirmations of Christian certainties in 5:13-21.

Writing on the style of 1 John, Peter Rhea Jones gave some interesting observations. He said that the letter contained tests for authentic Christianity. There are more than twenty tests in the course of five chapters introduced by four emerging patterns: "if we say" (1:5-10), "the one saying" (2:4-11), "everyone who" (2:23 to 3:12), "and the one" (4:12 to 5:12). According to Jones, John tested professing Christians, seeking to determine the real from the unreal. Examine carefully these four statements, and you will see that this is a prominent trait of the letter.[2]

In addition to Jones's observation about tests, he noted another trait of the letter. The writer of 1 John used a presiding metaphor throughout the work. This is a "master image which dominates a work."[3] The presiding metaphor of 1 John is "abiding in God." The expression occurs twenty-four times in five chapters. The Greek word for "abiding" is *meno*. It means a vital union and continuous communion with the Lord. Throughout the letter, the predominant idea is that union *(meno)* with God is the only basis for a relationship with the Lord. Continuous abiding in the Lord is the way to increase the believers' joy.

Now that we have examined some pertinent facts about this letter, such as author, occasion, purposes, and style, we are ready to study the letter itself. Remember that this letter came out of a real historical situation in the first century. It spoke to those times, and it speaks to our times. It was used in the first century to increase the joy. It still may help believers to increase their joy.

2
Jesus Christ Is Real
1 John 1:1-4

Ron Goulart's novel *Capricorn One* is a difficult story to classify. Either it is imaginative fiction or it is a serious attempt to deny the credibility of the American space program. *Capricorn One* is the story of a planned space trip to Mars. Soon after the countdown had begun, the mission had to be aborted because of a faulty life support system. To have scratched the mission would have ended the space program. The mission director convinced the astronauts to get out of the space capsule. Thousands of NASA officials then arranged for the astronauts to be moved to a large warehouse where mock space travel would be staged for the television audience. Finally, NASA officials announced a fabricated report of an accident where the three astronauts had been killed. The rest of the novel deals with the astronauts' attempts to escape NASA's captivity and to prove to the American people that they were alive.

On the surface, *Capricorn One* seems to be nothing more than imaginative science fiction. But somehow one might wonder if serious questions were being raised about the reality of space travel. After reading the novel, I asked myself, *Could these moon landings have been simulated somewhere on earth? Have human beings really gone to the moon?* Here I was raising questions of reality about events which happened in my lifetime. Over a decade has passed from the time the astronauts landed on the moon on July 20, 1969 to the appearance of such novels as *Capricorn One* and *Hangar Eighteen*. The latter also raises doubts about the reality of space travel. These doubts about credibility seem strange to us.

The farther away one gets from a historical happening, the more attempts there are to deny its reality. Less than fifty years after the life of Jesus on earth some people raised serious questions about the reality of Jesus. Time had elapsed since the gospel had been preached to and received by many people in the Roman province of Asia. In the course of the years, strange ideas infiltrated the minds of people. Some of these ideas questioned the historicity of Jesus Christ. A group of teachers known as Docetic Gnostics said Jesus could not have possessed a real body. They saturated the entire province with the idea that Jesus just seemed to have a body, that he did not really become a man. These false teachers existed for a time within the Christian church. This strange Docetic idea caused believers to wonder, *Was Jesus a real human being?*

Another group of teachers known as Cerinthians spread ideas denying Jesus' divinity. They got their ideas from Cerinthus, an Ephesian Gnostic. He said that Jesus was a normal human being born and reared in a normal way. According to the philosopher, divinity came on Jesus at his baptism and left him just before his crucifixion. This would have meant that Jesus only possessed divinity for approximately three years. This strange Cerinthian idea caused believers to wonder about the uniqueness of Jesus. They asked, *Did Jesus possess divinity only part of the time?*

Because the primary attack of these false teachers centered on the person of Jesus, John started his letter with amazing assertions about Jesus Christ (1:1-4). He began by saying that Jesus is the eternal Son of God, coexistent with the Father. In the same paragraph, John asserted that the Son of God was a real man. Few writers in the New Testament assert with greater intensity the reality that God became a man than John. His witness that Jesus was human centered on the fact of touching, hearing, and seeing the Lord. John started his letter with the theme—"Jesus Christ is real!" Throughout the letter, many other references testify to the uniqueness of Jesus' personhood and ministry.

Skepticism about Jesus Christ has abounded for over nineteen hundred years. Questions arise periodically about the humanity and the divinity of Jesus. Some can accept Christ's divinity, but like the Docetists of old they cannot bring themselves to acknowledge his humanity. Others can accept Christ's humanity, but they cannot accept the divinity of Jesus of Nazareth. In 1977 a group of theologians submitted essays in the book titled *The Myth of God Incarnate*. Some of the essays were types of *Capricorn One* which made readers wonder about facets of the reality of both the humanity and divinity of Jesus.

Being removed hundreds of years from the birth, life, death, and resurrection of Jesus could cause many questions. Did Jesus really become a man? If Jesus became a man, was he really the Son of God? With questions like these, we can look at John's assertion about Jesus Christ for answers. The letter begins with John's testimony that the eternal Christ became incarnate in Jesus. This Jesus did not just live over nineteen hundred years ago. This Jesus is alive confronting people today. Let us study John's divinely-inspired insights about Jesus of Nazareth.

The Eternal Christ

John's words about Jesus did not begin at Bethlehem. To talk about Jesus, John started from eternity. According to John, there has never been a time that Jesus has not been. John started with amazing affirmations about the eternal Christ: "from the beginning," "the word of life" (1:1), "the eternal life which was with the Father" (1:2). John's testimony described more than a great man. His words were about Jesus, the eternal and unique Christ.

Jesus existed before the incarnation. His birth in Bethlehem was not his beginning. The expression "That which was from the beginning" could have been a reference to creation, the beginning of history, the incarnation, or the beginning of the Christian message. A similar message is found in the Gospel of John: "In the beginning" (1:1). In the Gospel, John emphasized that Jesus existed before creation; in 1 John, the writer emphasized that Jesus existed before the incarnation.

Edward A. McDowell said that "beginning" denoted the

eternity and timelessness of Jesus.[1] Alfred Plummer stressed that the verb "was" *(en)* does not emphasize "came into existence" but "was in existence already." He emphasized that the verb was a "being verb" which conveys that Jesus existed from all eternity.[2] Before Jesus' historical manifestation, he existed. Since the words "which was from the beginning" precede the three other clauses ("which we have heard, which we have seen . . ., which we have looked upon and touched"), we should expect the meaning to precede these too. That is to say, before Jesus was heard, seen, or touched, he existed with the Father. This fact alone would declare a uniqueness. Ordinary human beings have a beginning. Jesus has *been* from the beginning.

John gave another expression to depict Jesus' preexistence—"the eternal life which was with the Father" (1:2). Again the verb "was" *(en)* is imperfect and expressed the Son's preexistence. The expression "which was from the beginning" (v. 1) stated Jesus' preexistence, and the expression "was with the Father" (v. 2) stressed that Jesus was coeternal with the Father. Jesus existed with the eternal God; in the course of time, God came to live in the arena of human existence. So John's first expression about the eternal Christ dealt with his preexistence.

John used three other expressions to describe Jesus as the substance of God's kind of life. The first one is "the word of life" (1:1); the second one is "the life was made manifest" (1:2); and the third one is "the eternal life" (1:2). The construction of "the word of life" means the word which consists of life. That means that when we look at Jesus we are looking at God. The expression "the life was made manifest" was the announcement that the eternal became incarnate. And, the expression "eternal life" means God's kind of life or the life which transcends earthly life. Jesus was the manifestation to the world of God's kind of life. Therefore, John made another grand assertion about Jesus. Not only was Jesus preexistent with the Father but he is also equal with the Father.

John was still not finished with insights into the eternal Christ. He used several phrases to depict the unique relationship of Jesus

Jesus Christ Is Real (1:1-4)

with the Father. Study carefully the following expressions: "which was with the Father" (1:2) and "with the Father and with his Son Jesus Christ" (1:2,3). John gave two fundamental truths of the apostolic message. The two truths were the distinctiveness of personality and the equality of the Father and the Son. John identified the eternal Son of God with the historical person of Jesus Christ. The repetition of "with" *(meta)* in reference to the Father and the Son mark emphatically the distinction and equality between the Son and the Father (v. 3).

To describe Jesus, John started in eternity. John R. W. Stott said that John's preface started with Jesus' eternal preexistence, progressed to his historical manifestation, and continued to the believers' joy in successive ages of history.[3] What a blessed insight about the Lord!

The Incarnate Christ

John continued with his testimony about Jesus of Nazareth. He had spoken of Jesus as the eternal Son of God. Then John stated that the eternal Son of God had entered time and had allowed himself to be known. When God became a man, he became much more understandable to human beings. Now let us examine John's insights into the incarnate Christ.

The fact that God became flesh is an incredible reality. "That which was from the beginning, which we have heard, which we have seen with our eyes, which we have looked upon and touched with our hands, concerning the word of life" (1:1). John used four relative clauses introduced by four neuter relative pronouns "which" *(ho)*. We have already said that the first clause, "which was from the beginning," was a reference to Jesus before his incarnation. The next three clauses relate how the eternal Christ became a human being capable of being heard, seen, and touched. The one who existed with God came to identify with human beings.

Sören Kierkegaard told the story of a prince who was single and wanted to marry a lovely maiden. Near his palace was a large city, and often he rode in his carriage to the city to take care of various duties for his father. One day, to reach a particular merchant, he had to go through a poor section. He happened to glance out of the window of his carriage into the eyes of a beautiful maiden.

The next few days, he returned to that section of the city—drawn by the eyes of the maiden. More than just seeing her, the prince had the good fortune of meeting her on two occasions. Soon he began to feel that he was in love with her. But he had a problem. How could he proceed to marry her?

Several options were available to the prince. He could order her to the palace and propose marriage. But even a prince wanted to feel that a girl wanted to marry him. Perhaps, he could go to her home and display his resplendent dress of royalty. No, the prince wanted a higher motive than "sweeping her off her feet" with flattery. Another option would be to masquerade as a peasant and try to gain her interest. He knew though that the act would be a trick.

Finally the real solution came to him. He would give up his kingly robes and move into her neighborhood. He would take up an occupation. During the day he would work and in the evening he would begin to share his time with her, discovering her interests and concerns. And in due time, should fortune be with him, he would win her love and marry her. This he did.

This simple story by the Danish theologian tells what God did. The eternal Christ took up residency with us. He left the splendor of heaven to come down to earth and win us. John's first exclamation was that the One who was from the beginning came where human beings could hear, see, and touch him. The incarnation of Jesus is incredible.

Not only is the incarnation incredible but it is also undeniable. John said people had heard, seen, and touched Jesus of Nazareth. The first clause refers to Jesus before the incarnation. The next three clauses refer to events of Jesus' life and ministry—"which we have heard, which we have seen with our eyes, which we have looked upon and touched with our hands." Two verbs are used for sight: *horan,* means to see (three times) and *theaomai* means to look

Jesus Christ Is Real (1:1-4)

intelligently so as to grasp the meaning and significance. Each experience of the human senses intensifies the undeniability of the incarnation. Notice the order: hearing, seeing, beholding, and touching. Seeing is greater than hearing, and beholding is more than seeing because it requires time and effort. Touching is even greater than hearing, seeing, or looking intelligently. Touching *(psēlaphaō)* means more than a casual touch. It means to examine closely. The apostles had no questions about the reality of Jesus' humanity. They had heard, seen, looked closely, and even touched Jesus. For them, the incarnation was undeniable.

The verbs in John's preface add to his report about the indisputable reality of the incarnation. There are four verbs in verse 1: heard, seen, looked, and touched. The first two, heard and seen, are in the perfect tense, suggesting the abiding possession which results from hearing and seeing. The last two verbs, looked and touched, are both aorists. They seem to refer to a particular time where the apostles had opportunity both to gaze thoroughly and to touch him. The last two verbs express an incontestable investigation by the observer. So John gave undeniable evidences for the incarnation.

After giving the incredible reality and undeniable evidences of the incarnation, John proceeded to say that the incarnation was a decisive act of communication on the part of God. In the incarnation, God expresses his deepest intention. "The life was made manifest, and we saw it, and testify to it, and proclaim to you the eternal life which was with the Father and was made manifest to us" (1:2). John used the word "manifest" *(ephanerothe)* twice. It means "to bring illumination" or "to make known." By means of the incarnation, God made himself known in a greater way than he had before. Because God became flesh, human beings could comprehend many qualities of his nature. Carlyle Marney in his book *He Became Like Us* describes the incarnation as God's attempt to explain himself, as well as to identify with the human plight.

John has given us two apostolic assertions about Jesus. First,

Jesus is the eternal Son of God who existed with the Father and was coequal with him. Second, the eternal Son of God became flesh. The event was incredible. It was attested by apostolic experience. Because he became like us, we can understand him. Hallelujah, what a Savior!

The Available Christ

John's affirmations about Jesus started in eternity before the incarnation. He proceeded to assert that the eternal Christ became the incarnate Christ whom the apostles heard, saw, studied, and touched. John's affirmations about Jesus did not stop with his earthly ministry though. John asserted that the Christ who lived on earth still lives and confronts human beings. Therefore, John was not just proclaiming the historical figure called Jesus, he was presenting the living Lord. The manifestation *unto us* (v. 2) becomes a proclamation *unto you* (v. 3). John believed that, throughout history, the Risen Christ was available for people to encounter and to experience.

John first described the apostolic actions of making Christ available. "We . . . testify to it" (1:2). "We proclaim also to you" (1:3). These are present tense verbs which suggest continuous action. Testifying and proclaiming were two apostolic actions of making Christ available. It involved a testimony and a proclamation. Testimony *(marturoumen)* involves an experience. To give a testimony, one must have been an eyewitness. The true witness is not one who has gathered secondhand information about Jesus, but one who has had a personal experience with him. Jesus, the one who came to earth, makes himself available so that people may experience him now.

Having a personal experience with Jesus gives one the authority to proclaim. The main verb of John's preface (1:1-4) comes in verse 3—"we proclaim" *(apangellomen)*. It is a present tense verb. The force of the tense suggests that John proclaimed Jesus. However, the proclamation of Jesus is not restricted to the first century. He may be proclaimed in every successive generation, for he is alive and confronting people with himself and his claims. Proclaiming Jesus is an action which asserts that Jesus is alive and available today. The Christ baptized in the Jordan, crucified on a cross, and risen from the grave makes himself available to people in today's world. We cannot just talk of Jesus existing in eternity or living in the first century; we must announce him as the One who is constantly available.

Christ makes himself available for special reasons. John mentioned two purposes of proclaiming Christ: "so that you may have fellowship with us" (1:3) and "that our joy may be complete" (1:4). The available Christ wants to establish "fellowship" *(koinōnia)*. When Christ was on earth, he created fellowship within the apostolic band. Take the time to read about Jesus and the twelve in the Gospel narratives. The fellowship was deepened by the coming of the Spirit at Pentecost. The fellowship was not limited to the first century. It has extended through the ages. The reason is because Christ is present with and in his people.

The word "fellowship" *(koinōnia)* literally means "having in common." Two or more persons may be said to have fellowship if they have something in common. James and John shared with Simon Peter the common pursuit of fishing (Luke 5:10). The believers' fellowship is the common participation of a union with the Lord. Because of this union with the Lord, the Holy Spirit indwells each believer; each one has the same Holy Spirit. This makes Christian fellowship mean much more than social, cultural, or recreational common interests. At the deepest level, fellowship means a union with the Lord. As a result of that union, believers belong to God and to each other. The common possession of God the Father, Son, and Holy Spirit makes the believers one body. The fellowship of the church means Christ's continuing presence with his people.

The objective of proclaiming Christ then was "so that you may have fellowship with us" (v. 3). People need a meaningful relationship both with God and with other believers in whom God resides. They have something in common. Fellowship in a church is not created with a meal in the fellowship hall or with a unanimous vote on an issue. Fellowship occurs when believers acknowledge the presence of God in their lives and seek to share the mission Christ intends. In John's day, the doctrine and behavior of the false teachers threatened to disrupt the church. The abiding Christ in believers produces a true *koinōnia*.

There was yet another purpose for proclaiming Christ: "that our joy may be complete" (1:4). This joy is that serene happiness which is the result of a vital union with the Lord. Joy began for John when he opened his life to Jesus. For over sixty years, John had continued to open his life to the Lord. His joy was increased as he continued to open his life to the Lord. John wrote his letter so that the joy of believers would be increased. Evidently some believers stopped with only a vital union. This brings a degree of joy, but joy is increased and intensified by a continuous and progressing opening of life to the living Lord.

The Christ is available to believers. He is the same One who existed in eternity. He is the One who lived, died, and rose from the dead. He is alive and available. It is not just his story believers hear. It is him! He is available to give us a fellowship with him and his people. Our Christian lives can be enriched infinitely with happiness as we open life more to the living Lord.

John's preface (1:1-4) is powerful! Its theme is Jesus Christ is real! It is more than a polemic against false teachers and their heresies. It is a positive assertion about Jesus Christ. The Lord existed with the Father from all eternity. He manifested himself in time and space with the limitations and traits of humanity. He is alive, confronting people in today's world. If people will open their lives to Jesus, he will join his life with them and will give both immediate and continuing happiness. The critics can never destroy the reality of Jesus Christ to one who has experienced him.

3
Taking Sin Seriously
1 John 1:5 to 2:2

Karl Menninger, the famous psychiatrist of the Menninger Clinic in Topeka, Kansas, wrote a book which focuses sharply on the concept of sin, *Whatever Became of Sin?* Menninger said that *sin* is a word which has been almost completely dropped from twentieth-century vocabulary. Menninger did not hesitate to relate sin to the selfish desires and ulterior motives prevalent in each human being.

The famed psychiatrist said that we have been playing a word game with the word *sin*. Rebellion, Menninger reported, has been replaced with the word *crime* or *delinquency*. Menninger also said that many attempts have been made to substitute the word *sick* for sin. This psychiatrist asserted that not all criminals are sick.

Menninger raised serious questions about the disappearance of absolutes needed to regulate life. Society has virtually discarded the Bible as having any authoritative bearing on life. Oddly enough, Menninger called for an examination of the biblical concept of sin—one which would include guilt, individual responsibility, accountability, and even punishment.

The writer of 1 John had not dismissed the idea of sin. He used the word *sin* either as a noun or as a verb nine times in eight verses (1:5 to 2:2). He also used other words which could be synonymous with sin, such as *darkness* and *unrighteousness*. The reason John dealt with the matter of sin early in his letter was because it destroys the believers' fellowship with God. Sin robs believers of the joy of intimacy with the Lord.

From the preface (1:1-4) we learned that one of John's reasons for writing the letter was for believers to have fellowship with the living Lord. This intimate fellowship with God is not possible when sin is present. Some false teachers in John's day claimed to be in fellowship with the Lord while living lives devoted to sin. John exposed the senseless claims of the false teachers. These false teachers refused to take sin seriously.

The structure of John's exposure of the false teachers becomes evident with close study of 1:5 to 2:2. First, John began with a great statement about the nature of God (1:5). Next, he introduced the claims of the false teachers with the expression "if we say" (1:6,8,10). Third, John denied the profession of the heretics with the expressions "we lie" (1:6), "we deceive ourselves" (1:8), and "we make him a liar" (1:10). Finally, John made three positive statements to refute the errors (1:7,9; 2:1-2).

Fellowship with God does not come on our terms. It comes on God's conditions. What then are God's conditions for us to have a close fellowship with the Lord? The Lord's conditions are to walk in the light, to confess our sins, and to aim for the ideal. Sin keeps us from fulfilling any one of these conditions, therefore, sin must be taken seriously. Let us examine closely the terms for fellowship with the Lord.

Walk in the Light

John introduced the subject of fellowship in 1:1-4. He indicated that the fellowship of believers exists only because of a union with God through Jesus Christ. The source of fellowship then is God, and the nature of God will determine the kind of fellowship. This truth accounts for John's declaration of the nature of God. The apostles learned from Jesus that God is light and that if his followers wanted fellowship with him they had to walk in the light.

From the life and teachings of Jesus, John learned a marvelous characteristic of God. "This is the message we have heard from him and proclaim to you, that God is light and in him is no darkness at all" (1:5). None of the other biblical witnesses tell us so much about

Taking Sin Seriously (1:5 to 2:2)

God's nature as John. In three striking statements, he gave insights into the character of God: "God is light" (1:5), "he is righteous" (2:29), and "God is love" (4:8).

There seem to be three main meanings to the expression "God is light." First, God's essential nature is to reveal himself. Just as it is the characteristic of light to shine, so it is the nature of God to disclose his nature. Second, God's essential nature is moral perfection. To reinforce this truth John added, "and in him is no darkness at all." Third, God's essential nature is unutterable majesty and splendor.

John's statement about God's character establishes the fact that those who claim to have a relationship with the Lord cannot be indifferent to morality. After this proclamation, John went to the inconsistent claim of the false teachers. It was the ridiculous claim to have a relationship with a God who is light and to walk in the darkness. "If we say we have fellowship with him while we walk in darkness, we lie and do not live according to the truth" (1:6). The false teachers asserted that sin (walking in the darkness) was a matter of no consequence. They said that it did not affect fellowship with God. The Gnostics treated righteous living with indifference, for the only thing that mattered to them was knowledge.

Sometimes people have the wrong idea of truth. John said that if people who claim to be advanced still walk in darkness they are not living according to the truth. Truth for the Christian is moral truth. Faith is not just an exercise of the mind; it is the expression of one's total life. Truth is both thinking and living. For the Christian, truth is something to be learned and obeyed. One cannot know the truth and walk in darkness at the same time.

Having refuted the inconsistent claim of the false teachers, John affirmed the consequence of being united with the Lord. "But if we walk in the light, as he is in the light, we have fellowship with one another, and the blood of Jesus his Son cleanses us from all sin" (1:7). To have opened life to God, who is light, is to lead a life of walking in the light. The verb "walk" *(peripatōmen)* is a Hebraism which depicts the totality of one's life-style—every attitude adopted, every word spoken, every decision made, every facet of living.

Walking in the light is possible because of a vital union with the Lord. "But if we walk in the light, as he is in the light" (1:7). Believers begin to walk the moment they open their lives to the Lord. Walking in the light also means fellowship with other believers. "We have fellowship with one another" (1:7). Having found the source of closeness to God, believers experience solidarity with others united in Christ. A closer walk with God will involve a closer walk with other human beings. Fellowship among Christians is both the result and expression of fellowship with God.

Walking in the light, then, means to experience the solution to the sin problem. "And the blood of Jesus his Son cleanses us from all sin" (1:7). The verb "cleanses" *(katharizei)* is in the present tense and suggests a continuous process. To walk in the light means that believers will be conscious constantly of sin. To walk in darkness means that we either ignore or deny the reality of sin. If we walk in the light, God has made provision in Christ's atonement to cleanse us from whatever sin would hinder our fellowship with him. The provision is "the blood of Jesus [Christ]." This is a reference to Christ's death. God treated sin seriously, for he gave his Son to cleanse people of their sins.

John's teachings are clear. People who have a relationship with God who is light will live lives of morality. They will treat sin seriously and apply God's provision continuously so that no barrier will be in the way of fellowship. John's idea is that if we are going to take sin seriously we must walk in the light.

Confess Your Sins

As we walk in the light, we become painfully aware of dark areas in our lives. To be in the presence of a person who has impeccable grammar makes one deficient in grammar painfully aware. Being with an immaculately clean and well-dressed person makes the disheveled, sloppily dressed individual feel deficient.

Taking Sin Seriously (1:5 to 2:2)

Likewise, when any human being comes into the presence of the absolute moral perfection of the Lord, there inevitably comes a painful awareness of the existence of sin. We cannot walk in the light of God's presence without becoming aware of our sins.

Oddly enough, the false teachers made an absurd claim. They claimed that they were past sinfulness. "If we say we have no sin, we deceive ourselves, and the truth is not in us" (1:8). Their first claim (v. 6) was to have fellowship with God and to disregard morality. Their second claim was the ability to be so enlightened that they did not have sin in their lives. They denied the fact of sin. These false teachers had Gnostic tendencies: sin was a matter of the flesh and did not defile the spirit of a person. They didn't consider sin a real problem, for they didn't feel they were guilty of any sin.

Walking in the light brings an awesome awareness of sin. To claim "we have no sin" was simply self-deception and refusing to accept the truth of God's word. The attempt to deny one's sin is common. We want to explain sin away with such ideas as social disease or psychological illness. Furthermore, we go to great lengths to explain our sin so that guilt can be resolved.

The proper way for a Christian to treat sin is not to deny it, but to admit it. "If we confess our sins, he is faithful and just, and will forgive our sins and cleanse us from all unrighteousness" (1:9). The act of confessing means to say the same thing about ourselves that God says. And what does God say about us? He says that we have sinned and that we fall short of his great intention. He also lists the numerous ways we express this rebellion against his intention. So, instead of establishing that we are sinless, we ought to confess our sins.

Confessing our sins will mean that we give sin harsh treatment. Confession requires honesty. Many of us are not willing to say about ourselves what God says. Confession also requires a dependency. It means that we cannot bear the burden of sin. Confessing is calling God into our lives to help us with the burden of sin. Confession will also involve receiving forgiveness. Sin hinders the relationship with God. Confessing our sins leads to reconciliation.

To whom should we confess? John R. W. Stott, in an excellent book titled *Confess Your Sins: The Way of Reconciliation,* gives the insight that confessions could be made to God, to an offended individual, to the church, or to a minister. Stott gave examples of times when one should confess to God and to the others. He concluded that primary confession should be made to God. The writer of 1 John had God in mind as the recipient of confession. The personal pronoun "he" of 1 John 1:9 refers to God.

Knowing that we are to confess to God leads to another question, What kind of God do we confess? John described God as "faithful" and "just" with regard to sinners confessing their sins. He is "faithful" refers to the fact that God will keep his promise of mercy to the penitent. He is "just" in his dealings. This means that God, who is moral perfection, cannot remit sin lightly. He deals with sin on the basis of redemptive work. When a person confesses sins, God will be true to his character. God's mercy and justice are ultimately one. We are forgiven because of who God is.

What does God do when we confess our sins? According to John, God "will forgive our sins and cleanse us from all unrighteousness." The first phrase implies that sin is a debt which God remits, and the second phrase implies a guilt which he removes. This forgiveness and cleansing are conditioned upon confession. To confess to God is to have the debt of sin remitted and the guilt removed.

Confessing our sins means that we treat sin seriously. The closer we get to God, the more we are aware of the sins in our lives. The darkness must not be denied or repressed. It must be confessed. Confessing our sins to God on a regular basis will be a positive step in taking sin seriously.

Aim for the Ideal

John wanted his readers to have a serious view of sin. The readers were confronted with strange ideas about sin. False teachers claimed, in effect, "You can have a relationship with God without a real concern for morality" or "you have reached such a level of

Taking Sin Seriously (1:5 to 2:2)

attainment that sin is no longer a problem in your life." John was concerned about these attitudes toward sin. To combat these claims, John said, "Walk in the light" and "Confess [your] sins."

The false teachers came up with a third heretical claim: that they had never sinned. That claim contradicts the consistent witness of divine revelation and denies the truth of human experience. God's verdict on the human race is that "all have sinned" (Rom. 3:23). To deny that we have sinned is to deny blatantly God's word. The person who denies having sinned lives without the instruction of God's word. "His word is not in us."

John made the fact of sin in a person's life an explicit claim. "If we say we have not sinned, we make him [God] a liar, and his word is not in us" (1:10). No one could or can claim to be without sin. John had been careful in telling how to deal with sin. He had told his readers to walk in the light and to confess their sins. John then presented another way to deal with sin, to aim for God's ideal. God will not lower his standards for sinful human beings. He will not lessen the tension between what we are and what we ought to be. So, John wrote to give the believers God's ideal. "My little children, I am writing this to you so that you may not sin" (2:1). The teaching is clear. God's ideal for every believer is a sinless life. God never says, "Be good half the time. Or, be good three-fourths of the time." God always says, "Be good all the time." His standard is perfection, 100 percent. The goal is "that you may not sin."

Only one person has reached the ideal, Jesus. So the gospel is grace too! Without grace, God's ideal would be an insurmountable obstacle which would drive us to despair. The demands of the Lord make us aware of our failures. We desperately need his grace. The gospel is always demand and grace. God constantly says, "Sin not." But at the same time, he says, "If any one does sin, we have an advocate with the Father, Jesus Christ the righteous" (2:1). Our lives are always in tension with what God wants and what we are.

The believers need to aim for the ideal. The Christian pilgrimage is the joyful journey of letting go of sin and taking up God's kind of life. How do we take up the slack between the ideal and actual? John gave the answer, "We have an advocate with the Father, Jesus Christ the righteous" (2:1). The word "advocate" *(paraklēton)* describes someone summoned to assist another. It was used in law courts to describe a person who represented someone at a trial. A good translation of the word would be "helper." The "advocate" or "helper" means that God identifies with behavior and gets involved in moving us toward his goal.

Only Jesus Christ is qualified to help Christians move from where they are to where they ought to be. Notice how John gave the Lord's qualifications for helping with sin. "And he is the expiation for our sins, and not for ours only, but also for the sins of the whole world" (2:2). The word "expiation" means that God has done something in Jesus Christ to help with the distance between God and man. In the King James Version the word "expiation" *(hilasmos)* is translated "propitiation." Outside biblical usages, the word *hilasmos* was often used to describe an offering made to placate the anger of an offended god. However, in New Testament usages, the word seems to convey the Old Testament concept of an offering for sin. It describes what God did to remove the alienation between God and humanity. God did not need to be reconciled. People needed to be reconciled to God. Only Jesus has the qualifications to remove that alienation. He is qualified in character. He is qualified in action, for he defeated the last of human enemies with his death and resurrection. By the Lord's unique ability, he can help take us from where we are to where we ought to be.

Our day differs culturally, socially, politically, and scientifically from John's day. But the reality of sin hasn't changed. Modern people treat sin lightly. Many who believe in the reality of God think that he makes considerable allowances for our sin. The message of God's desire for perfection is not taken with sufficient seriousness. John's message is not obsolete. Sin needs to be taken seriously. Look at God's character, and it will help you to walk in the light. Stop denying or avoiding the reality of your sins and confess them to God. Aim for the ideal with the idea that the Helper will move you gradually and constantly to where God wants you to be.

4
Becoming Better Believers
1 John 2:3-11

Most human beings have a desire to be better. Only a few people do not want to improve their character, their skills, and their life-styles. Business persons want to achieve excellence in their vocations. They often attend meetings and seminars about their particular projects, tips on salesmanship, or ideas about motivation. After long years of formal education, doctors seek to improve their practice of medicine; dentists attend seminars to learn the latest techniques of dental hygiene; and lawyers attend conferences to learn the latest laws which affect their practices. Church leaders also attend conferences to learn skills which would enhance their ministry in the church.

In addition to becoming better vocationally, people seek to achieve excellence in their recreation. Amateur golfers seek constantly to find techniques which will lower their scores. With the rising interest in tennis, Americans are seeking to acquire skills in tennis. Those who enjoy fishing also constantly search for better baits and new techniques which will help land the big ones. The desire to achieve excellence or to be better seems to be a trait of most human beings.

John wrote his letter to increase the believers' joy. Without a doubt, remaining in a static position of the Christian experience brings frustration and unhappiness. Christians cannot be happy remaining as they are. Christians can only be happy when they are becoming better believers. But the question arises, How does one become a better believer? In John's day, strange ideas circulated about achieving excellence. Some said, "Gain more knowledge."

As noted in previous chapters, Gnosticism had infiltrated the Christians. Gnostics advocated some special knowledge of esoteric myths. Though this idea does not circulate under the name of Gnosticism today, many say the way to become a better believer is, "Study religion. Read the Bible." Of course, reading and studying the Bible are profitable exercises; but an atheist can memorize Scripture passages and study biblical facts.

Others in John's day said, "Deny yourself." They emphasized asceticism. They claimed to do without certain things which they felt enhanced their relationship with God. Today one does not have to listen carefully to hear people stating the many refusals a person has to make in order to be a better Christian. To be sure, quitting bad habits is helpful, but the Christian experience is more than quitting bad habits. It is a relationship with the Lord.

Then there were those in John's day who doggedly insisted that to get better Christians had to add good deeds constantly to their lives. They said, "Do more and you will be better." John taught that obedience came naturally from a relationship. Adding rules would be an endless process, and adhering to legalistic regulations will not enhance being.

John's letter is relevant to today's churches. There seems to be an authoritative stance in most evangelical congregations about how to become a Christian—"The just shall live by . . . faith" (Hab. 2:4). But there seems to be a relativism about how to become a better Christian. All kinds of demands are made as guides for growth—attend church services, tithe, read the Bible, witness every day. These are great activities which result from a relationship with God not from a set of rules. Let us study carefully John's inspired ideas about becoming better believers.

Obey Christ's Commands: 1 John 2:3-5

John began his instructions to the believers by telling them that achievement came in the Christian experience by obeying the commands of Christ. Getting better as a Christian comes out of relationship. The way to be sure of a relationship with the Lord is to

Becoming Better Believers (2:3-11)

notice whether you obey Christ. Many people claim a relationship with the Lord, but the profession does not guarantee an authentic relationship with the Lord. Only when people obey the commands of Christ do they prove their relationship.

On the surface, John's teaching seems to advocate both legalistic claims and esoteric knowledge. Closer examination will dispel these interpretations. John used the word "know" in a relational manner. He did not use the word "know" in the Gnostic manner, such as knowledge which came from mystical experiences or from the accumulation of facts. John used the word "know" *(ginōskomen)* to mean knowledge gained by experience.

Let me give you an example which will distinguish the difference in usages of "know." For many years my favorite preacher has been Leonard Griffith. Over my ministerial career, I read about him. I studied his sermons. I mastered the contents of his nineteen books. Consequently, I knew Leonard Griffith in an academic manner. In 1976, this renowned preacher came to our seminary campus to preach for a week. It was my pleasure to meet him at the airport, to listen to him in the chapel, to visit with him for many hours, and to eat with him. I came to know Leonard Griffith in a different way. The latter was an experiential knowledge. Previously I had known about him, but I came to know him personally.

John's usage of know was based on personal knowledge. Intellectual knowledge about Jesus Christ is not enough. Many people know about Jesus' birth, his good life, his marvelous teachings, his death on the cross, his resurrection, his ascension, and his promised return. Yet, just to know the facts is not enough. *To know the Lord* means to come to a time where you open your life to him. You know him in an experiential manner. Throughout the letter, John gave various expressions for the experience of a Christian: "fellowship . . . with the Father and with his Son Jesus Christ" (1:3); "fellowship with him" (1:6); and a favorite expression, "we know him" (2:3). The expression "we know him" is a present tense verb which denotes an experience which leads to a progressive knowledge.

Knowing the Lord personally will inevitably lead to obeying his commandments. "And by this we may be sure that we know him, if we keep his commandments" (2:3). John was not talking about a burdensome adherence to legalistic regulations. He was speaking about an obedience which grows naturally and spontaneously out of a relationship with the Lord.

Let us think for a moment in a practical manner about obedience growing out of a relationship. In a genuinely happy marriage, there is a relationship between two people. The marriage is more than a legal transaction. It is a relationship. Now let us think of a situation within the marriage. The wife is going to have to be away from the home for several days to visit her parents. The wife writes some "commands" on a list which the husband needs to do in the course of the week. The husband does not observe these rules out of a burdensome obligation. He obeys them because of a relationship. That is the reason the Christian obeys Christ's commands, from a personal knowledge of Jesus Christ.

"He who says, 'I know him,' but disobeys his commandments is a liar, and the truth is not in him, but whoever keeps his word, in him truly love for God is perfected" (2:4-5). Profession is tested by obedience. If a person claims to know Christ and disobeys his commands, that profession cannot be trusted. The person's conduct contradicts his profession and proves it to be false. Yet, the person keeping Christ's word is shown to be a true Christian. True love for God is expressed not in sentimental language or mystical experience but in moral obedience. The proof of love for God is loyalty to Christ's commandments. The word "commandments" is one of John's favorite. It is a word which includes the sayings and teachings of Jesus Christ. It could refer to the whole of God's revealed will.

We want to be better believers. Growing in the Lord depends upon an initial personal knowledge. We come to know the Lord through an act of personal faith. After this initial knowledge comes increased knowledge. This is not intellectual knowledge, but experiential knowledge as we continue to open our lives to the Lord. We

Becoming Better Believers (2:3-11)   43

come to know Christ better, and this results in obedience to his commands.

Imitate Christ's Life: 1 John 2:6

John continued his instructions to the believers by telling them that achievement came to the Christian experience by imitating Christ's life. Many people profess to be Christians, but the reality of their faith can be seen in their Christlikeness.

John used relational expressions to describe the state of the believer. He used "fellowship" in 1:1-4 and "walking in the light" in 1:5 to 2:2. John increased his relational expressions in 2:3-11. Notice these expressions "to know him" (v. 3), "to be in him" (v. 5), and "to abide in him" (v. 6), "By this we may be sure that we are in him: he who says he abides in him ought to walk in the same way in which he walked" (2:5-6). By such expressions, John denoted the close communion or relationship between believers and the Lord.

The expression "in him" is descriptive of a union with the Lord. The expression "abides in him" *(menein)* is one of John's favorite expressions. It means that Christ lives in believers. It also implies habitual fellowship. The imitation of Christ's life will come as a result of being united with the Lord. The phrase is similar to that in John 15:4 where Jesus said, "Abide in me, and I in you. As the branch cannot bear fruit by itself, unless it abides in the vine, neither can you, unless you abide in me." We need to be careful to think of the relationship before we talk of the obligation. We cannot live like Jesus until we are united with him and live in habitual fellowship with him.

Having established that obligation comes out of a relationship with the Lord, we are prepared to look at the obligation. The obligation is obvious—"to walk in the same way in which he walked." The word "walk," as noted earlier, means the whole round of life's activities. John used a strong demonstrative pronoun, "that one," *(ekeinos)* for Jesus. *The New English Bible* translates the expression "to live as Christ himself lived." It would have the idea of "he—that man there." The importance of following or imitating Christ is prominent in the New Testament. "For I have given you an example, that you also should do as I have done to you" (John 13:15). "Because Christ also suffered for you, leaving you an example, that you should follow in his steps" (1 Pet. 2:21). The word "example," which Peter used, is *hupogrammos* which is a combination of two Greek words meaning "the writing above." Students learned to write by copying the writing above. Christians learn to live by imitating the life lived by Jesus of Nazareth.

The life of Jesus provides the pattern for believers' lives. John did not give a concrete description of the life of Jesus in his letter; he assumed that his readers were familiar with the life of Jesus.

Nothing would help believers more than a careful study of the life of Jesus. The character of God has been manifested in the earthly ministry of Jesus. Looking carefully at Jesus' life-style will disclose the pattern we are obligated to live. Think about a few traits of Jesus' life: tempted at every point of human vulnerability but resisted; criticized severely but moved forward; performed selfless service to humanity as demonstrated in his miracles; listened carefully and understandingly to people; did not practice retaliation when he was reviled; forgave people when he had been injured; never committed a rebellious act; never said an idle word. Jesus deserves to be our example, for he is absolutely perfect.

Looking carefully at Jesus' example might cause us to ask, Can I really live as Jesus lived? Some say that the example is too great, and they won't even try. Others say that the example is superb, and they will try. Then after trying in their strength, they find that imitating Jesus' life is an impossibility. To live as Jesus lived requires a divine dynamic. Therefore, the believer has the pattern for living and the power to live as Christ lives. Christ abides or lives within the believer to help move him or her toward the example of Christ.

Let's illustrate this truth. Suppose I have a deep desire to be an accomplished tennis player. I would go and study the skills of a professional player, such as John McEnroe. If I studied him carefully for one year and tried to imitate his moves, could I become a professional? Of course the obvious answer is no. To have the ability of John McEnroe, I must possess some of his skills within me. The believer can imitate Jesus, for he lives within. The believer does not have to struggle for Christlikeness. The believer has to open more of life to the Christ who lives within. This action will result in becoming a better believer.

Practice Christ's Love: 1 John 2:7-11

John concluded his instructions to the believers by telling them that achievement came in the Christian experience by practicing Christ's kind of love. Again John based action upon a relationship. He used the relational expression "which is true in him and in you." Love is made actual by a relationship with the Lord. The way to be sure of this relationship is to see if you practice Christ's kind of love with people. Many claim to love, but the reality of love may be seen in actions. Only when people love as Jesus loves do they prove their relationship of being in Christ or of walking in the light.

John had been talking in general terms when he spoke of keeping Christ's commandments and walking as Jesus walked. He became more specific when he spoke of loving. Maybe this commandment to love includes all the other commandments of Jesus. George Findlay said love is "*the* commandment" of the letter of 1 John. Also, the act of loving could describe the totality of Jesus' life. He loved God, and he loved his neighbor as he loved himself.

John made some curious statements about the command to love. It is described both in terms of oldness and in terms of newness. "Beloved, I am writing you no new commandment, but an old commandment which you had from the beginning; the old commandment is the word which you have heard. Yet I am writing you a new commandment" (1:7-8). The commandment to love was an old one. The believers had heard the command since the beginning of their Christian experience. It was not invented and issued by John. The command to love was a prominent feature of

Jesus' teachings. For centuries before the Christian era, the command to love was embedded in the Mosaic law (cf. Deut. 6:5; Lev. 19:18).

Nevertheless, this command to love had a newness about it. How could one say that this commandment was new? The word "new" *(kainos)* often meant new in kind, as well as time. The command to love is new in the sense that Jesus gave a new quality to it. No one ever loved as Jesus loved. It is a new command in the sense that every aspect of the Christian life is new. It belongs to the new age, the age in which the darkness is passing away and the real light is shining. For people to love one another in a self-giving manner is something new which occurs in the new order of things.

Another curious statement about the command to love is its actualization in Jesus' life and in the lives of believers. "Which is true in him and in you" (v. 8). The concept of love was not rhetoric from Jesus; he practiced love. This, too, was the newness of the commandment. "A new commandment I give to you, that you love one another; even as I have loved you, that you also love one another" (John 13:34). The love of Jesus was a different kind of love. No person had ever demonstrated this type of love. In Jesus people know what true love is.

William S. Taegel, in his book *People Lovers,* described God's kind of love. He said there were three kinds of love. First, there is "if love" which is a conditional kind of love. Second, he said there is a "because love" which results as a responsibility. Third, he said there is an "anyhow love" which is a love that loves irrespective of the person or the deed. God's love is an "anyhow love."

The same kind of love which Jesus possessed can be practiced in his followers. Believers have a vital union and intimate fellowship with the Lord. Consequently, the Lord shares his kind of life with each believer. This will mean that believers possess God's kind of love which is a self-giving love. It is a love which wills to seek the highest good of an individual.

The response to the commandment to love discloses the character of an individual. People who refuse to love show that they belong to the darkness. "He who says he is in the light and hates his brother is in the darkness still" (2:9). "But he who hates his brother is in the darkness and walks in the darkness, and does not know where he is going, because the darkness has blinded his eyes" (2:11). God's character is light and love. Failure to share God's love means not to share his light. If love means light, hate means darkness. If we love people, we see how to love them.

John made the point clear again with the expression "he who says" in verses 4,6,9. In verse 4, the person professing to be a Christian must obey Christ's commandments. In verse 6, the person claiming to be a Christian must imitate Christ's life. In verse 9, the person professing to be a Christian must practice love. When we are in the light, we will practice love.

Becoming better believers begins with becoming Christian. To be a Christian is to open one's life to Christ. Being Christian begins when the Lord joins his life with our lives. The attainment or betterment of believers occurs when they continue to open more of their lives to Jesus Christ. Allowing Christ into our lives and continuing a fellowship with him opens the possibility of keeping his commandments, imitating his life, and practicing his love.

5
Spiritual Passages
1 John 2:12-14

Gail Sheehy wrote a book entitled *Passages: Predictable Crises of Adult Life*. Her book drew extensively from the works of Erik Erikson and Daniel Levinson, two men who have written on the normal psychological development of adults. Sheehy's unique contribution to the stages of adult life was her interviews with 115 educated, middle-class people between the ages of eighteen and fifty-five. Her book is a popular treatment of various predictable "passages" in the saga of adult existence.

The apostle John wrote about the different spiritual passages of Christians. In 1 John 2:12-14, he mentioned the stages of little children, fathers, and young men. Before we study this section, some preliminary facts might be helpful. First, John gave two sets of three parallel statements, the second mainly repeating the first. Second, John used the present tense "I write" in the first set of statements and the aorist tense "I wrote" in the second series. Third, John designated the stages of the Christian experience with the terms "little children," "fathers," and "young men."

The repetition of the statements in different tenses—"I write . . . I wrote"—is difficult to explain. Robert Law suggested that John wrote the first set (2:12-13*a*) in the present tense, and he was interrupted. After some delay, the apostle came back to complete his letters and repeated what he had said in verses 12-13*a*. Some commentators think that the last set in the aorist tense (2:13*b*-14) referred to a former letter, and those in the present tense referred to the present letter. Most New Testament scholars explain the use of the two tenses in 1 John as a matter of stylistic variation. The aorist of the second trio is probably an "epistolary aorist" which has the same effective meaning as the present tense for stylistic purposes. The Revised Standard Version translators used the latter and translated the present and the aorist both as "I write."

John divided his readers into three groups whom he names "little children," "fathers," and "young men." He addressed each group twice. Why did John use these three groups? Some say that John used the term "little children" to embrace all believers. Then, they say, John divided the believers into two groups, namely fathers and young men or the mature and the immature. Other scholars say that John had different chronological ages in mind. John R. W. Stott and F. F. Bruce, two competent New Testament scholars, say that John was not indicating physical ages but stages of spiritual development. God's family, like the human family, has members of different levels of maturity. These three groups seem to represent different passages of the spiritual pilgrimage.

Within every church there are people in different spiritual passages. The "little children" are those who have come recently to the knowledge of God and to the forgiveness of sin. Chronologically, these people may be twelve, twenty, or seventy. The "young men" are those who are bearing the brunt of the church's spiritual welfare. They are developing into strong and victorious believers. The "fathers" represent those within the fellowship of a church who possess the depth and stability of mature Christian experiences. Our study of these spiritual passages will focus on the topics of newcomers, becomers, and overcomers.

Newcomers: 1 John 2:12-13c

The spiritual passage begins with the new birth. It is the beginning of the Christian life, and it represents an exciting time in the spiritual passage. We shall look at the little children or the newcomers from both sets of statements. "I am writing to you, little children, because your sins are forgiven for his sake" (2:12). "I write to you, children, because you know the Father" (2:13).

John used two words to address the little children or new-

Spiritual Passages (2:12-14)

comers. In verse 12, he used the word *teknia*; and in verse 13, he used *paidia*. Both are translated "little children." John R. W. Stott gave the unique distinction of the two words. John's use of *teknia* was an emphasis on the relationship between the nature of the child and the parent. The word *teknia* comes from a word which means to beget or to give birth. The idea in the word is that a child will possess the nature of the parent. So, the emphasis is on the kinsmanship of the believer with the Heavenly Father. John used the second word *paidia* to emphasize a child's subordination to the parent. Thus, the newcomers were addressed as "little children" who have been begotten by God and who lived in subordination or dependence upon the Heavenly Father."[1]

A Christian first experiences the Lord and receives divine forgiveness. "Your sins are forgiven for his sake" (2:12). The experience of forgiveness is the initial moment of acceptance into God's family. The word "forgiven" *(apheōntai)* is a powerful word. The verb translates a perfect tense denoting the fact that their sins were forgiven at a point in the past and remained forgiven. The word translated "forgiveness" was used in a variety of ways. It could refer to the cancellation of a debt. When we incur a debt, we must pay it. Without being too transactional, we see that human beings are indebted to God to the extent that we cannot pay. Therefore, the Lord has to help us with our debt. He cancels the debt.

Forgiveness also refers to the removal of a stain. Here "forgiven" was used as a metaphorical reference to guilt. The expression means that sin leaves a person with guilt. To have forgiveness means that God lifts the guilt from a person and takes it away.

Forgiveness could also refer to the restoration of a relationship. When we sin, we erect a barrier called alienation before God. Jesus came to break the barrier and to establish a relationship with erring human beings and a holy God. Forgiveness, then, is a great first experience that means our sin debt has been canceled, our guilt has been solved, and a relationship with God has been established.

The first experience of a Christian was also described by John as a beginning knowledge. "You know the Father" (2:13). The verb "you know" is a perfect tense, and it refers to the fact that believers came to know the Lord at some point in the past and remain in that relationship. I remember when I first came to know the Lord. It was an exciting time. It was the beginning of a pilgrimage. I was a newcomer to the kingdom of God. I rejoiced that I had been forgiven and that I had fellowship with the Lord.

In every church there are newcomers of all ages, people who have been forgiven and been born into the kingdom. They have the characteristics of children: a sense of wonder and amazement over their new experience; a sense of bubbling excitement; a state of dependence upon the Father; a deep realization of their need for instruction. Nothing will enhance liveliness in a church more than newcomers to the kingdom.

No spiritual passage is to be static or stationary. It is to be dynamic and progressive. We cannot keep the status of a newcomer. To remain in a passage brings real problems. As much as we desire, we cannot restore the looks and feelings of youth. We must accept the aging process and be willing to move to the next passage. Likewise, the spiritual newcomer cannot be new always. There needs to be growth. Nothing hurts the fellowship of a church in the same way than having converts who refuse to pass beyond infantile, simplistic Christian experience. Newcomers must inevitably progress to becomers.

Becomers: 1 John 2:13*a*,14*a*

The spiritual passage needs to continue. Our joy will not be full if we try to remain newcomers. Our joy may be increased by moving to the passage of a becomer. The joy of the Christian experience is increased as we move from where we are to where God wants us to be. John addressed a group in the church whom he called "fathers." These were the people who had moved away from the gate to venture into the pasture.

The "fathers" John addressed were the spiritually mature in the church. "I am writing to you, fathers, because you know him who is

Spiritual Passages (2:12-14)

from the beginning" (2:13) and "I write to you, fathers, because you know him who is from the beginning" (2:14). Those Christians had forgiveness of sin and an initial knowledge of the Lord. They had progressed in their relationship with the Lord. The fathers, as a result of life's experience, had come to know the Lord in many situations and ways. At the beginning of their Christian passage, they knew the Lord in conversion, but the passing of years and their trust in the Lord had resulted in a greater experiential knowledge of the Lord. They had moved from the status of newcomers to becomers.

Keith Miller wrote an interesting book on the Christian life called *The Becomers*. He stressed that conversion for the believer was only a beginning and not an arrival. The convert has been freed to start actualizing the gifts and potentialities which have always been inherent in his life. The Christian is to think of himself as a "becomer" in process.

Having established the fact of whom the "fathers" represent, we may now face another significant question. How do we achieve maturity? Does the passing of years guarantee spiritual maturity? Of course not. Some chronologically young people demonstrate spiritual maturity, and some older in age reflect spiritual immaturity. If age does not bring spiritual maturity, how do we move into the passage of a becomer?

Answering the question about how to achieve maturity is bound up with John's expression, "you know him." The process of becoming is bound up with the initial beginning of the Christian life. We cannot become until we begin. The word "know" *(egnōkate)* refers to an experiential knowledge. It is the initial act of opening life to the Lord. That is the beginning. The force of the verb "you know" refers to an experience in the past which continues to the present. Growth takes place as believers continue to open their lives to the Lord. The knowledge of the Lord ripens with continuing experiences with the Lord. The "fathers" had progressed to a point of a deep communion with the Lord.

John used another expression to describe the becomers. "I

write to you, fathers, because you know him who is from the beginning" (2:14). "Little children" or newcomers get to know God as their Heavenly Father. The becomers live their lives in communion with God. They have come to know him "who is from the beginning." More than likely this expression was a reference to the immutable, eternal God who does not change as we change with the passing of years. God remains the same yesterday, today, and forever. Therefore, another hint is given about how to move into the passage of a becomer. The answer is to continue to live in fellowship with the unchanging, living Lord through the varied experiences of life.

Passing through different experiences in fellowship with the Lord brings maturity. It moves us from newcomers to becomers. Knowledge in John's thinking came as a result of experience. The "fathers" had experienced acceptance by God. They had fought with the satanic solicitations. They had passed through the trials and vicissitudes of life. They had faced their fears and anxieties with God's help. They had gone through valleys of despondency, frustration, and anxiety with God's help. Each experience brought them into closer fellowship with the Lord. Living life in fellowship with the Lord had increased their joy and developed maturity. Going through the struggles probably led John to think about another group in a spiritual passage.

Overcomers: 1 John 2:12,14*b*

The spiritual passages through which believers pass vary. They are not necessarily chronological. In the spiritual pilgrimage, there will be a stage of struggle. Our joy will increase as we learn to overcome the evil one. John addressed a group in the church whom he called "young men." These were people busily engaged in the battle with the evil one. The people in this spiritual passage may be called the overcomers.

Each Christian goes through the passage of an intense struggle with the evil one. "I am writing to you, young men, because you have overcome the evil one" (2:12) and "I write to you, young men,

Spiritual Passages (2:12-14)

because you are strong, and the word of God abides in you, and you have overcome the evil one" (2:14). The Christian life is not just enjoying the excitement of initial conversion and the stability of sustained fellowship. It also means the action of fighting the enemy. Believers have forgiveness from past sins, but they need deliverance from the present power of the evil one. There is the reality of conflict in the believers' lives, and so there is the spiritual passage where they can be overcomers.

Living the Christian life involves an intense struggle with the evil one. The masculine form of "evil one" *(ponēron)* indicates that John referred to Satan. Throughout the Bible, Satan is presented as one who seeks to oppose the will of God. Applied to the "young men," Satan seeks to oppose constantly what God wants to happen in every believer's life. And what does God desire? The Lord wants his character to be formed in every believer. "That we may present every man mature in Christ" (Col. 1:28). When a believer seeks to grow in Christlikeness, the evil one opposes. So to be a Christian is to be in opposition to the evil one.

Believers need not despair about the struggle with the evil one. They have an assured standing with the Lord. Again the verb "you have overcome" is in the perfect tense, and it indicates the present consequences of a past event. During his life and ministry, Jesus overcame the evil one. Because Jesus overcame the evil one, believers enter into this victory. When a person opens life to Jesus, he allows the victorious Lord to enter.

Not only do believers depend upon a past event but also believers have the resource of a present experience. "You are strong, and the word of God abides in you." To speak of the word of God abiding in the believer was to suggest that God lived permanently within the believers. His presence is the secret and source of daily victory over the evil one. This is the reason believers can be overcomers. They conquer because they are strong, and they are strong because God lives in their lives. So long as we trust in God's power and not in ourselves we may rejoice in victory.

The Christian life has many passages. Some in the church are new believers. They are excited, and they need to grow in wisdom and knowledge. Others are involved in the struggle with the evil one as they seek to grow in Christlikeness. Still others enjoy the maturity of growing in knowledge through varied experiences with the Lord. John gave a beautiful description of the church in verses 12-14. Within every congregation are newcomers, becomers, and overcomers.

6
Coping with a World System
1 John 2:15-17

The young man caught my attention as I preached. He was handsome, well-dressed, and he had the physique of an athlete. What caused me to focus on him was his apparent, deep interest in the sermon. When the worship service ended, I greeted people and exchanged pleasantries. The young man came to me, introduced himself, and proceeded to tell me some facts about himself. He was a student at the university. He shared with me the exciting fact that he was a new Christian. While I rejoiced with him over that fact, he stunned me with a question: "Preacher, I am glad to be a Christian. But how do you expect me to cope with the world system in which I live?"

I asked, "What do you mean?"

He said, "I mean that I have a hard time being a Christian. My family gives little attention to the church. Most of my fraternity friends are not believers. Also, it seems the whole world does not respect Christ's principles. Could you give me some help in coping with this world system?"

The young man's question perplexed me. Maybe the reason arose out of the fact that I, too, have a hard time coping with a world system. What could I tell the young man which would help him? Three options came immediately to my mind. The first possibility was to tell the young man to escape the world and live a semi-monastic life. Some believers join monasteries, and others choose to try to live apart from the world in some type of separation. The second possibility was to tell him not to fight the opposition. Give in to the pull of the world, and there would no longer be a struggle.

This is why churches are full of "worldly Christians." Of course, I related quickly to the young man that neither of these two options were biblical. Then I presented a third option. Live in the world but not of the world. Stay in the family, the fraternity, the university, and the friendships, and live before the watching world a Christian life. To live in the world system we need God's help.

The writer of 1 John recognized that believers had a hard time coping with the world system in which they lived. Christians experienced the indwelling Christ, but they had to live in a hostile environment. Paganism was rampant in the first century. Vicious corruption, extending to every aspect of life, was the pagan world's hallmark. Lust, avarice, bribery, pleasures, and disdain for human life were socially acceptable. Honesty, chastity, compassion, and unpretentious living were disdained. Believers had a difficult time because the world was so degraded and the Christian community was so small. Coping was difficult.

John turned from a description of the church (vv. 12-14) to a description of the church in the world (vv. 15-17). He gave instructions to the struggling believers about their attitude toward the world. God's people enjoy forgiveness from sin, fellowship with God, and conquest over the evil one, but their confrontation with a world system is not over. Christians must live in the world as God's called, chosen, and Spirit-filled persons. The Christian's experience with the world cannot be a cloistered one or a conforming one. To help us cope with this world system, let us examine John's insights.

Exhortation Against Love of the World: 1 John 2:15

John began his helpful hints about coping with a world system with a terse exhortation: "Do not love the world or the things in the world. If any one loves the world, love for the Father is not in him" (2:15). The exhortation was addressed to loyal members of the church whose spiritual status was unquestioned. John warned the believers against an attitude which could lead them to spiritual destruction, namely love for the world.

What did John mean when he used the word "world"? The

Coping with a World System (2:15-17)

word occurs six times in verses 15-17, and it appears several times later in the letter. Probably "world" was one of the most used terms in the Johannine vocabulary. John had several usages for the word. At times, though it was a minor usage, John utilized the "world" to describe the created universe (cf. John 1:10). John also used the word to denote the world of people. It was used to depict the human population, such as "God so loved the world" in John 3:16. This usage of "world" refers to the human race collectively.

The third major usage of the word was one which had a moral dimension. It was the most common usage in John's writing. This usage of "world" was a collection of people in rebellion against God and, therefore, characterized by all that was in opposition to God. This was what might be called "the world system." It involved the world's values, pleasures, and aspirations.

John's exhortation provided a means of coping with an evil world system. When John said "love not the world" (KJV), he thought of an affection. The expression "love not" is an imperative. It is a strong command. The word "love" in the imperative was used in a different way than in other places throughout the letter. In other places, John used love to refer to affection for God or to self-giving compassion and care. It was used in the sense of a love that was concerned for the benefit of the person loved. In this incident, John's thought was on the pleasure which the person hoped to get and not to give. To love, in this sense, would mean to be attracted by something and to want to enjoy it for selfish gratification. So, John's command to "love not the world" (KJV) was an exhortation against a super selfishness, the kind of selfishness which destroys self and others.

John's exhortation was grounded upon the fact that love for the world and love for the Father are incompatible. This follows clearly John's usage of "world." To love the world as John used the word was to give affection to what is opposed by God. Love for the world and love for God are mutually exclusive. Believers cannot cope with a world system by trying to give their affection to their Father and to the hostile, pagan world. To survive in a jungle of paganism, the believer's affection needs to be directed to God. John's first therapeutic advice was an exhortation, "Do not love the world!"

Investigation into the Nature of the World: 1 John 2:16

John proceeded to explain more fully his rather authoritative exhortation. He made a thorough investigation into the world system. John picked up on the phrase "the things in the world" (v. 15) and elaborated on the nature of the world. "For all that is in the world, the lust of the flesh and the lust of the eyes and the pride of life, is not of the Father but is of the world" (2:16). C. H. Dodd said: "In a few telling phrases he (John) characterizes what seem to him the essential marks of the pagan way of life."[1] To John, the pagan world system consisted of three elements: the lust of the flesh or base desires, the lust of the eyes or false values, and the pride of life or egotism.

Nothing will help us cope with a world system more than to investigate seriously the precise nature of the world. To know the world for what it is will help us relate to it. The first characteristic of the world system is the lust of the flesh or base desires. The term "flesh" includes all of the desires and appetites which are centered in human nature and exercised without regard to the will of God. The word "lust" is a morally neutral word which generally means "desire." Only the context determines whether the desire is good or bad. In John's usage, in verse 16, the meaning is clearly a negative desire. John used the term "flesh" in the sense of humanity using God-given desires for self-gratifying reasons. Therefore, the nature of the world is to give in to the basic desires of the flesh.

The world system builds an outlook oriented toward the self. Persons who follow the idea of the world system use human desires to pursue their own ends. John looked at the pagan world and saw people taking God-given human desires and using them in ways to gratify self or to exploit people. The world takes the good things of God and uses them for self-gratification. The world constantly seeks to take the God-given desires and utilize them in a way which

Coping with a World System (2:15-17)

pleases their human desires rather than God's will. William Barclay described the lust of the flesh as follows:

> It is to make a god of the pleasures which are purely worldly pleasures. It is to live a life which is dominated by the senses. It is to be gluttonous in food; effeminate in luxury; slavish in pleasure; lustful and lax in morals; selfish in the use of possessions; regardless of all the spiritual values; extravagant in the gratification of worldly, earthly, and material desires. The flesh's desire is forgetful of, blind to, or regardless of the commandments of God, the judgment of God, the standards of God, and the very existence of God.[2]

The second characteristic of the world system is the lust of the eyes or false values. C. H. Dodd described this as "the tendency to be captivated by the outward show of things, without inquiring into their real values."[3] This means the desire for beauty divorced from the desire for goodness. Eve was attracted to the forbidden tree. Achan looked at the forbidden spoils of Canaan. David looked upon Bathsheba for the sake of her beauty and not her goodness. All of these are examples of unlawful cravings which entered the eyes. The world is captivated by the outward show of things. The world system looks upon the external beauty rather than the inward reality.

The third characteristic of the world system is the pride of life or extreme egotism. The Greek word for "pride" and "life" are worthy of investigation. "Life" *(bios)* comes from a word which means "the things which support life." "Pride" *(alazon)* means a braggart. It refers to the braggadocios who exaggerate what they possess in order to impress other people. The world system has people who seek to impress everyone with nonexistent importance. C. H. Dodd gave an abridged translation of a passage in Theophrastus *Characters* (Number 23).

> The *Alazon* is the kind of person who will stand on the mole and tell perfect strangers what a lot of money he has at sea, and discourse of his investments, how large they are, and what gains and losses he has made, and as he spins his yarns he will send his boy to the

bank—his balance being a shilling. If he enjoys company on the road, he is apt to tell how he served with Alexander the Great, how he got on with him, and how many jewelled cups he brought home; and to discuss the Asiatic craftsmen, how much better they are than any in Europe—never having been away from Athens. He will say that he was granted a free permit for the export of timber, but took no advantage of it, to avoid ill-natured gossip; and that during the corn shortage he spent more than fifteen hundred pounds in gifts to needy citizens. He will be living in a rented house, and will tell anyone who does not know the facts that this is the family residence, but he is going to sell it because it is too small for his entertainments.[4]

The pride of life is self-aggrandizement over surface matters. The participants of a world system have the desire to shine or to outshine others.

To cope with the world system, the believer needs to understand pagan society with its sensuality, superficiality, and pretentiousness. These are characteristics of a world order which is not under the lordship of Christ. The Christian cannot cope by seeking loyalty both to God and to the world. The two orders are mutually exclusive. Base desires, false values, and egotism are not from the Father. These traits do not show likeness to God's character, and these qualities are contrary to what God wants for his people. The Christian should choose to live in an identity with the world but a separateness from it.

Verification of Superiority Over the World: 1 John 2:17

The believers needed more than an exhortation against loving the world and an insight into the nature of the world. The believers in Asia Minor needed an assurance that Christianity was superior to the world system. John verified the superiority of God's way over the world. "And the world passes away, and the lust of it; but he who does the will of God abides forever" (2:17). So many times believers in the power of a world system get to a place where the world's way seems superior to God's way. John needed to give a word of hope and assurance.

God's way is superior because of the transitory state of the world. "And the world passes away, and the lust of it" (2:17). The use of the present tense points to the fact that the process of dissolution is already at work. Many people give their lives totally to the gratification of human desires. They live on the level of satisfying desires. When one desire is satisfied, it has to be satisfied again when the desire arises again. Living life in satisfying human desires can get meaningless and mundane. Life consists of more than satisfying human desires.

The things which attract our eyes are also in the process of passing away. Many people devote their lives to the pursuit of things which are only attractive to the eyes. They do not consider what is really valuable in life. Observation alone should teach us that those things which attract our eyes are transitory. Beauty fades. Money leaves us quickly. The honors we receive are soon forgotton. Material goods depreciate and deteriorate. The world is passing away, and those things we once saw and valued are sought no more.

The egotism of the pagan world is also in the process of passing away. Those who play "make-believe" with life will realize the falsehood and the emptiness. Braggarts one day will awaken to the fact that they do not outshine others. The pretentiousness is not permanent. The world is passing away.

John's readers found great assurance in the words "and the world passes away." They lived amid pretentious luxury, rampant sensuality, gross inhumanity, and exaggerated materialism. The majority of the population indulged in these pagan ways. The small, Christian community often wondered if they were right in their beliefs and practices. John verified to them the superiority of the kingdom of God over the world system.

Affirming the impermanence of the world was only a half assurance. John assured his readers further: "He who does the will of God abides forever" (2:17). Permanence belongs to the person who does the will of God. To belong to the world system means death and destruction. But to belong to the new order of God's kingdom means to belong to something enduring and everlasting.

The best way to cope with the world system is to live in it and do the will of God. Doing God's will means that we take the longer look and we see the permanence of God's way.

The question, How can I cope as a Christian in a world like this? is, indeed, a difficult one. There is the strong tendency to live for the moment, to be attracted to the external, and to live in a make-believe world. John's words have been helpful. To cope with a world system he directed our affection toward God and away from the world. He let us see the characteristics of the world system, and he told us the permanence of doing God's will. With these insights and verification, we can live with greater optimism amid the evil world system.

Of course, two of the greatest coping powers are the indwelling Holy Spirit and the Christian community. The Holy Spirit lives within believers to give them victory over the world. Also, the Christian community provides a support group. With those truths from John, with the Holy Spirit within us, and with God's people about us, we can cope with any world system.

7
Will the Real Christian Please Stand?
1 John 2:18-27

Since the beginning of television, game shows have had a popular appeal. One of the long-running programs was *To Tell the Truth*. It was hosted by two outstanding game show personalities, Bud Collyer and Garry Moore. For over two decades this game show interested audiences. The host had a special guest who had something unique about his or her life. Two other guests appeared and claimed the same identity. The panel members on *To Tell the Truth* were well-known celebrities, and they proceeded to question each guest. They sought to identify the real person from the two impostors. After the panel members questioned the guest and guessed who the real person was, the host would say: "Will the real _____ _____ please stand?"

In John's day there were impostors in the church. Many people claimed, "I am a believer." Yet, as their lives were examined closely, they possessed strange ideas about Jesus Christ. Some of them claimed to have a knowledge of Christ, but they denied either his humanity or his divinity. Furthermore, many of the impostors disdained their fellow human beings. They did not demonstrate Christian love. These impostors created unhappiness in the churches of Asia Minor. The real believers were confused and robbed of their full joy. John called these impostors "antichrists." Throughout the letter of 1 John, the apostle applied three tests: A real Christian believes that Jesus is the Christ; a real Christian walks in the light; a real Christian loves other human beings. Upon examination, using these tests, of people who professed Christianity, the statement could be made, "Will the real Christian please stand?" Only those who could pass these tests would be considered real believers.

From the contents of 1 John 2:18-27, we see that the author was driven to write this letter. The apostle had worked long and hard in the churches of the Roman province of Asia. Now his work was in jeopardy. Some church members had seceded from the main body. They had set themselves up as a rival Christian church. By belief and conduct, they had completely separated themselves from the Christian gospel, as handed down from the apostles and proclaimed and practiced under John's guidance. Bewilderment prevailed about who were the real Christians. Using definite distinctives of believers, John described the characteristics of real believers to his readers (2:18-27). A real Christian continues in the faith, possesses an anointing, and believes that Jesus is the Christ.

Thousands of people belong to churches in today's world. But membership in a local congregation is not conclusive proof of a real Christian. C. H. Dodd says that "formal membership is no guarantee that a man belongs to Christ and not to Antichrist."[1] Withdrawal was a sure proof that the false teachers in John's day never shared in the real life and fellowship of the Christian communion. Otherwise, they never would have fallen away. Churches have been filled with people who profess Jesus Christ, yet church buildings are empty and Christ's ministry goes lacking. How can we determine the real from the unreal in today's world? We cannot use church membership or mere profession. We shall have to use John's measurement of determining the real Christian.

Perseverance: 1 John 2:18-19

John began his discrimination between the true and the false by drawing a clear distinction between the impostors and the genuine Christians. A clear distinction between the real and the impostor involved the matter of continuation with Jesus Christ. Many people will profess faith in Jesus Christ, but John made it clear that the true disciple can be detected by a perseverance. John made a sharp distinction between the real and the unreal by calling the impostors "antichrists" (v. 18). Furthermore, he distinguished sharply between

Will the Real Christian Please Stand? (2:18-27) 67

the *they* who left and the *us* who remain (v. 19).

The prevalence of many impostors signaled to John that the church was at a critical point in her history. "Children, it is the last hour; and as you have heard that antichrist is coming, so now many antichrists have come; therefore we know that it is the last hour" (2:18). John had witnessed many crises in history—the fall of Jerusalem, the persecution of the Jews, the beginnings of Roman persecution with Nero, and many others too numerous to mention. For the first time in John's life, a widespread heresy threatened the survival of Christianity. Some people professed to be a part of the church, but some of the group denied Christ's divinity and others denied his humanity. According to John, the prevalence of the impostors had to mark "the last hour." John thought this doctrinal problem was the immediate prelude to the consummation of the age.

Some nineteen hundred years have passed and history still continues. Was John wrong? Could one say that John was mistaken? No, John viewed history in a different manner. The new age dawned with Christ's coming. The age to come had come in Jesus Christ. The last hour had struck. The time between Christ's first appearance and his final appearance are "the last days." John, and other believers of the first century, expected Christ's imminent return. They felt that the present moment contained the possibility of being that moment when history would be brought to a climax.

John's main concern was the prevalence of impostors of Christianity whom he called "antichrists." The term "antichrist" appears only in John's letters (1 John 2:18,22; 4:3; 2 John 7). But it was the expression of the Old Testament concept of a person or people opposed to God. Throughout the history of God's people every time there arose a great evil which seemed to be setting itself against God and against his people the tendency was to think of this in a personalized anti-God force or the supreme enemy of God. For example in 168 BC Antiochus Epiphanes, king of Syria, sought to eliminate the Jews and to destroy their worship. He invaded Jerusalem and killed thousands of Jews and sold thousands into slavery. He erected an altar in the Temple court to Zeus, and he sacrificed a pig on the altar. Some referred to Antiochus as the "abomination of desolation" (see Dan. 11:31). He was an anti-God force. Later, Caligula the half-mad Roman emperor wished to set up his image in the holy of holies in the Temple. The Jews also felt that this was an anti-God force at work.

Paul referred to some anti-God force in his Thessalonian letter. He spoke of "the man of lawlessness" as one who exalted himself above God (2 Thess. 2:3-4). John mentioned the false teachers, the heretics, the impostors as the anti-God for, indeed, they were. In 1 John, the "antichrist" is identified in terms of the specific situation confronting the churches. The fact is that "antichrist" is not so much a person as a principle. This is the principle which is hostile to God. Instead of one "antichrist," there were many "antichrists." These were the false teachers who denied the reality of the incarnation or the reality of the divinity of Jesus. These false teachers professed to be a part of the church, but they were separated from those who believed that Jesus is the Christ. Whether the secession was formal or whether this was a doctrinal wall is not certain. Nonetheless, the true believers could be identified by John by their continuation with Christ.

The impostors may be seen by their departure from the church. "They went out from us, but they were not of us; for if they had been of us, they would have continued with us; but they went out, that it might be plain that they all are not of us" (2:19). The false teachers had not been voted out of the church; they departed voluntarily. Their departure was a disclosure of their true identity. It was the discovery of the counterfeit, the pulling off the mask to see the real identity.

The departure of the false teachers did not mean that they once possessed eternal life and lost it. John made it explicitly clear that "they were not of us." They had only been apparent members. Membership in a church is no guarantee that a person belongs to Christ and not to "antichrist." External membership is no proof of union with the Lord. The departure of the group demonstrated that their profession was empty.

Will the Real Christian Please Stand? (2:18-27)

Reading John's statement about departure causes us to think seriously about the church. Many people confess to be Christians by means of their church membership. But either by beliefs or behavior, serious questions arise about the reality of the professions. When persons depart from the church, the falsity of their professions becomes apparent. There are signs today of impostors. They have departed from the Christian fellowship, for they never were really a part of it.

A sure sign of a real Christian is one who remains or continues with Christ. Steadfast persistence in God's way is commended throughout the biblical record. Look and see if one stays "by the stuff." Spectacular beginnings are not the important things. It is those who hear the Word and bear fruit, not those who endure only for a while. Those who remain demonstrate that their knowledge of Christ is more than intellect. It is a continuing experience with the Lord. It is a vital union and daily communion with Christ. Because Christ lives within believers, he helps them to persevere. So the real Christian will continue. But there is another measurement for determining the real Christian.

Anointing: 1 John 2:20-21,26-27

John continued to seek to distinguish between the true and the false. Another clear distinction between the real and the impostor involved the matter of a divine anointing. Many people will profess faith in Jesus Christ, but John made it clear that the true disciple has a distinctive anointing by God. "But you have been anointed by the Holy One, and you all know" (2:20). The word for "anointed" is *chrisma* which means an anointing. It is translated "unction" in the King James Version. The "you" is emphatic and could be translated "you too." John was making a contrast between the impostors and the true believers. Maybe the heretics claimed to have received their superior knowledge of divine things in a special ceremony of "anointing" or initiation similar to that of the pagan mystery religions. John said, in effect, "You too have an anointing, but yours is a genuine anointing, for you have received it from God."

The word "anointed" *(chrisma)* may be a deliberate pun on the word "antichrist" *(antichristos)*.

What does the word "anointed" *(chrisma)* mean? C. H. Dodd has an unusual interpretation of "anointed." He said that the anointing refers to the Word of God which teaches the truth to believers. Because the believers had received the Word of God, they had come to know the truth, and therefore they had the antidote to false teaching. Dodd's idea of *chrisma* comes from a Hellenistic or pagan background.[2]

According to most views, the word "anointed" *(chrisma)* had a strong Hebrew background. In the Old Testament the act of anointing with oil was a ceremony in which priests and prophets were consecrated to their high office. When the Messiah (Christ) came, he was anointed not with oil but with the Holy Spirit (Luke 4:18; Acts 4:27; 10:38). It is likely, therefore, that the anointing which we have received from God is the same Holy Spirit. If the false teachers or impostors were "antichrists," there is a sense in which believers have the Christ.

So, John said to his readers that at the time of their conversion they were consecrated with the Holy Spirit. Perhaps this interpretation could be substantiated with John's words which came later in the letter. "But the anointing which you received from him abides in you, and you have no need that any one should teach you; as his anointing teaches you about everything, and is true, and is no lie, just as it has taught you, abide in him" (2:27).

Paul had used the term *chrisma* in relation to the gift of the Spirit. "But it is God who establishes us with you in Christ and has commissioned us; he has put his seal upon us and given us his Spirit in our hearts as a guarantee" (2 Cor. 1:21-22). Paul used three terms to describe the bestowal of the Spirit upon a believer—*chrisma, sphragis,* and *arrabon.* John used the first *(chrisma)* to assure his readers that the real believer has the anointing of the Holy Spirit, and the impostor may have all kinds of anointings but not from the Holy One.

Will the Real Christian Please Stand? (2:18-27)

Each true believer has the gift of the Holy Spirit. This is his or her anointing. Maybe several questions arise about the Holy Spirit. Who is the Holy Spirit? According to the Word of God the Holy Spirit is God himself. The word *paraclete* of 1 John 2:2 could mean that the Holy Spirit is Christ's other self. Another prominent question is, When does the Holy Spirit come to reside in a believer? Well, since the Holy Spirit is "Christ's other self," he comes when one opens life to Christ. What does the Holy Spirit do when he comes to abide in a believer's life? The Holy Spirit comforts, guides in truth, assures troubled hearts, and teaches. So, each true believer has the Holy Spirit because he or she has opened life to Christ.

Having established that the "anointing" refers to the gift of the Holy Spirit, we are ready to discuss a prominent result of the anointing. In verse 20 John said, "and you all know." The King James translation has, "ye know all things." The best reading is "you all know." In the Old Testament, only selected people were anointed and given God's Holy Spirit. The Asian heretics claimed that special knowledge of divine things came only to a select coterie. But, to the contrary, John said that all believers have this knowledge. Saving knowledge is not the privilege of a select elite but of every genuine member of God's kingdom.

What did John mean by "you all know"? Does it mean that believers possess facts of technical scholarship? Of course, it doesn't mean that. John used the word "know" *(oidate)* not in the sense of intellectual information but a personal experience. This knowledge is an initial relationship with God and a continuing fellowship with the Lord. This is the kind of knowledge which could be the possession of every person. By means of a personal experience with the Lord, the individual receives the insights necessary to live a life that will be worthy of the new relationship.

John added a word of assurance about this knowledge or personal experience with Christ. "I write to you, not because you do not know the truth, but because you know it, and know that no lie is of the truth" (2:21). What John said was people who utter heretical statements indicate that they are not possessed of the divine anointing. The impostors could be detected from the real by the results of a divine anointing.

Belief: 1 John 2:22-25

John had been presenting ideas which would help distinguish the true from the false. He had presented the idea that the true could be determined by their perseverance and by their anointing of the Holy Spirit. The third measurement which John used was belief about Jesus Christ. The fundamental test of the professing Christian concerns the view of the person of Jesus. Impostors either deny the humanity or divinity of Jesus. Real Christians affirm that Jesus is the Christ. Real Christians do not stop with confession but proceed to abiding. The truth is, therefore, their belief rests not only in confession of facts but also an intimate relationship with Christ.

Look at the statements about the Christ. "Who is the liar but he who denies that Jesus is the Christ? This is the antichrist, he who denies the Father and the Son. No one who denies the Son has the Father. He who confesses the Son has the Father also" (2:22-23). The first statement is a denial of Jesus. There were those in John's day who denied the divinity of Jesus. The writer spoke of those who deny "the Son," and it is likely that he regarded "Christ" and "Son" as equivalent terms. To be specific, these people were Cerinthians (see ch. 1). Some of these followers accepted Jesus as a man but denied that he was the Son of God. Docetists confessed their belief in the Christ but denied the reality of the incarnation. They could not confess that Jesus was a human being. These were those who said that Jesus only seemed to have a body.

As a result of denying Jesus was the Christ, John could fittingly say that their attitude was that of "antichrist." To John, the height of heresy was to deny that Jesus is the Messiah, the Son of God, and the Savior. To reduce Jesus to a mere man or to allow less than full indwelling of divinity is to strike at the root of Christianity.

Modern thinkers have sophisticated and refined means of stating similar denials about Jesus. Recently, the British Broadcast-

Will the Real Christian Please Stand? (2:18-27)   73

ing Company put out a film entitled *Who was Jesus?* It was written by theologian Don Cupitt. The figure of Jesus was as tenuous as the photography was splendid. The film presented denials of Jesus' virgin birth; Son of God status; and resurrection. This is a view held by influential persons in churches today. G. A. Wells wrote two massive books to say that Jesus of Nazareth never existed but is the creation of the minds of the first century. Add to these "Christian" denials the disbeliefs of those who embrace other religions, and you have a condition akin to John's day. There are many who deny Jesus either as a man or as the Son of God. So, the confession that Jesus was either not human or divine, according to John, came from the impostors.

The second confession came from the real Christians. "He who confesses the Son has the Father also" (2:23). This is the confession that the historical Jesus is the Son of God. The question Jesus put to his disciples, "Whom say ye that I am?" (Matt. 16:15, KJV). is the fundamental question put to every generation. John's answer was, "Jesus is the Christ." To confess that Jesus is the Christ has several meanings. It means that we believe God came to earth in the human Jesus. He was baffled by life's mysteries, tempted, and lonely. His tears and his laughter were not playacting. His pain in Gethsemane was real, and his suffering on the cross led to death. To confess Jesus as the Christ is to affirm his humanity. But this confession also affirms Jesus' divinity. It acknowledges that Jesus was God himself. He lived a perfect life. The real Christian has a powerful confession that the human Jesus is the Son of God.

Belief in Jesus consists of more than reciting statements about the humanity and the divinity of Jesus. It means an intimate relationship with Jesus. John spoke of allowing Christ to abide in us. "Let what you heard from the beginning abide in you. If what you heard from the beginning abides in you, then you will abide in the Son and in the Father" (2:24). John began with an emphatic expression, "and you." This sets the real believers over against the impostors. Generally speaking the expression "what you heard from the beginning" refers to the gospel message, but specifically the reference is to the truth concerning Jesus. John's emphasis was on union with Christ. The word *abide (menein)* describes a person in spiritual union and in intimate fellowship with the Lord. "And this is what he has promised us, eternal life" (2:25). The concept of "eternal life" is another term for abiding in the Son. It is God's kind of life. The person who believes Jesus is the Christ has God's kind of life.

John presented a way to examine all professing Christians through three questions and answers. Is there a perseverance? The impostors have departed, and the authentic believers have continued with Christ. Is there an indwelling? The false prophets have their human anointing, and God's people have an anointing of the Holy Spirit. Then the last question comes, Is there a belief that Jesus is the Christ? The heretics deny the humanity or the divinity of Jesus. The real believers confess that Jesus is the Christ, and they live in vital union and in constant fellowship with the Lord. Now John says in effect to each generation, "Will the real Christian please stand?"

8
A Letter from the Father
1 John 2:28 to 3:3

Some of my treasured experiences have been those times when I received a letter from my earthly father. His letter writing to me began when I went away to college. He did not write frequently, but each letter had a specific purpose. I can remember that some of his letters were friendly reminders to stay with the books. Other letters were stimulating encouragements to a homesick boy. Maybe there were two or three letters of mild reprimand for being too free with the gasoline credit cards. Most of the letters were responses to my request for money. Those brief notes with enclosed checks were my favorite. After college Dad's letter writing continued—compliments for marrying such a good girl; information about family, sports, or business; and on occasion a letter of apology for losing his temper with me. Whatever the occasion, a letter from my dad was a treasured experience.

John had endeared himself as a spiritual father to the churches in and near Ephesus. When he wrote to these churches, his favorite address to them was "little children." The expression was suggestive of both the author's advanced years and of the affectionate, tender relationship which existed between him and the believers in Ephesus. John called the believers either *paidia* "children" in 2:18 or *teknia*, "little children" in 2:1,12,28; 3:7,18; 4:4; 5:21. On occasions John added the possessive adjective as in 2:1 "*My* little children" (author's italics). Therefore, when the readers received a letter from the beloved apostle John, it was like a letter from their father.

John, the beloved pastor, had some important matters to discuss with his spiritual children. His letter of 1 John is filled with many instructions, warnings, assurances, and promises for his children. In this study of 1 John 2:28 to 3:3 we shall focus on the idea of a pastor, namely John, writing to his people. In this section he gave several general insights for his children. Let us read John's words to the believers of Ephesus. Without a doubt, there will be a word of God for us.

The Confidence of God's Children: 1 John 2:28

John realized that many life situations both in their secular environment and in the church could intimidate God's children. The false teachers could cause some believers to lose their confidence. John, therefore, sought to build the confidence of believers.

The origin of confidence comes from abiding in Christ. "And now, little children, abide in him" (2:28). As stated in a previous chapter, the word "abide" was a favorite term of John's. It appears twenty-three times in 1 John, seven of those times in 1 John 2:18-28. Abiding in Christ means an initial union with Christ, as well as a continuing communion with the Lord. The word helped to assure the children that they were united with Christ and his presence was continuously with them. John wanted his readers never to forget the presence of Christ. If believers never celebrate or acknowledge the presence of the Lord, and if Jesus is just a perpetuated memory to us, we shall continue to be frightened. Our confidence will be shattered. But if during our days on earth we live consciously in the presence of Christ, we shall have a confidence. Nothing will assure us and lessen our fears more than the conscious realization of Christ's presence. It builds confidence.

In addition to the realized presence of Christ, another confidence was given to the believers. This involved the coming revelation of Jesus Christ. Christ is present now, but he will be present in a greater way in the future. "And now, little children, abide in him, so that when he appears we may have confidence and not shrink from him in shame at his coming" (2:28). John used two words to describe the final return of the Lord, "appears" *(phanerō)*

A Letter from the Father (2:28 to 3:3)

and "coming" *(parousia)*. The verb "to appear" had already been used by John to describe the Lord's incarnation (1:2). The word conveyed the thought of the invisible becoming visible. Jesus appeared the first time so that the hidden Word of God could become flesh. The Lord is hidden from view now, although he is present with his believers, but one day he will become visible again from heaven. The Lord's return will mean the personal presence of one absent.

The other word used to describe the Lord's final appearance was "coming" *(parousia)*. This word was used for the visit of a ruler to some part of his dominion, an occasion for celebration and rejoicing. Even today people turn out in great numbers when the president of the United States makes a personal appearance. This is the kind of atmosphere which is conveyed by this word: the return of Jesus to this world in visible splendor, like a reigning king. Christ's return should give great confidence to the believers, for his return assures them of resurrection from the dead, the gathering of Christ's people, and the apportionment of final destiny. Jesus is coming, and his advent should spell outstanding hope and optimism for believers. The Lord's return will mean the return of the King of kings to earth.

People react to the Lord's coming in one of two ways. Some will have confidence. Others will shrink from the Lord in shame. Confidence *(parrēsia)* occurs in 3:21; 4:17; 5:14. Literally, it means "frankness of speech." It described the Christian's boldness of approach both to people as a witness and to God as a suppliant. The thought is the confidence with which a person may enter into the royal presence and speak without fear or intimidation. To those believers who are in union and communion with the Lord now, the final return of Jesus will be a natural continuation of a present relationship.

Those who will be ashamed when the Lord comes will be either those who are not in union with him or those who are not in communion with him. In that day if a confession of Christ has been a mere external, formal one, the Lord will say, "I never knew you" (Matt. 7:23). Only if, in a lifetime of deepening devotion, we abide in him, shall we be able to anticipate with confidence to hear the Lord say, "Come, ye blessed of my Father" (Matt. 25:34, KJV).

God's children in today's world face hostility, animosity, and ridicule from modern impostors or "antichrists." We should not be flustered or fearful. We shall increase our joy when we abide in Christ's presence and we anticipate his visible presence.

The Character of God's Children: 1 John 2:29

John could not refrain throughout his letter from mentioning the character of God's children. Some New Testament scholars think John's train of thought was interrupted. He had been speaking of the Lord's coming, and he then mentioned God being righteous as well as his children being righteous. John was not rambling. His thoughts were on his readers being God's children, and he moved his thoughts to their character.

John talked about the character of the Heavenly Father. "If you know that he is righteous" (2:29). There is an abrupt change of persons between verse 28 and verse 29. The "little children" and "he" of verse 28 changes to God as the subject in verse 29. Believers know as fact some great truths about God. They know that "God is love." They also know that "[God] is righteous." The term "righteous" *(dikaios)* refers to correct moral behavior. John knew that to understand God's children one needs to look at their Heavenly Father. This is true of the earthly family. Children, by heredity and environment, have the nature of the parents. The Heavenly Father is "righteous," morally perfect. Whatever God is, he is holy or just. Whatever God does, he is right. That God is righteous is a biblical axiom. "The Lord is righteous, he loves righteous deeds" (Ps. 11:7). The Father is righteous, so we would expect his children to be righteous and to practice righteousness.

Character for God's children results from a spiritual birth. John introduced a new idea when he used "born of him." Natural birth comes by means of human parents. It relates us generally to the human race and specifically to two people, namely a mother and father. The physical birth produces physical, mental, and emotional

A Letter from the Father (2:28 to 3:3)

likenesses in the child. But there is another birth. Those who open life to God are "born of him" *(gegennētai)*. They become children of God. Their character is like his character. They perform deeds or actions like his deeds or actions. John wanted his readers to know that their character did not come by their works, ritual, or by words but by a vital union and communion with the Lord.

Behaving in accordance with God's character distinguishes us as his children. "You may be sure that every one who does right is born of him" (2:29). John stressed that righteousness was a consequence of the spiritual birth. Of course this does not mean that all moral people are God's children. The readers could take comfort in the fact that if they did what was righteous it was a sure sign that they were born of God. Since it is God's nature to be righteous, it must be the nature of his children to be and to do righteousness. A person's righteousness is the evidence of the new birth, not the cause or condition of it.

The only way persons have to prove that they are believers is the righteousness of life. Professions of union with the Lord will always be proved or disproved by the practice of life. The professing Christian cannot have much joy when righteous living is not observed. Yet, joy may be made full when profession of Christ who is righteous is matched with a believer who lives righteously. In John's letter, Christian character—its origin, standard, and manifestation—was never far from his mind. Character must consume the thoughts of God's children.

The Completion of God's Children: 1 John 3:1-2

John had other words to write to God's children. He wanted the believers to glory in their present status as God's children, but he also wanted them to anticipate the future of God's children. The child of God represents a new kind of person which will help make a better world. Yet, the child of God never reaches ultimate maturity on earth. The child/Father relationship finds its fulfillment in the future.

Maybe to understand the completion of God's children, we

ought to start where John started. He started with the commencement of the Christian life and the continuing pilgrimage. Listen to John: "See what love the Father has given us, that we should be called children of God; and so we are (3:1). John used the term "children" not "sons of God," for he reserved the term "Son of God" exclusively for the only-begotten Son. The term "children" suggests that a new kind of people have emerged.

When the prodigal son came to himself in a far country, he realized that he had really never been a son. It was not until he returned home and entered into a filial relationship with his father that he became a real son. Just so, God created human beings in his image. He gave biological life and the potential for spiritual life. But, until a person chooses, he or she will be God's creatures but not his child. Without a doubt there was exclamation and surprise when the father made the prodigal a son.

Likewise, there is amazement and surprise when the Heavenly Father accepts a returning prodigal. "See what love" in 1 John 3:1 meant originally "of what country." It is as if the Father's love is so unearthly, so foreign to this world that he wonders from what country it may come. The term "children of God" is not just a name. It is a character. "So we are" is an expression which speaks of being. God who created us has begotten us and we share in his nature and life. We really are his children. There is breathless wonder over this new kind of relationship.

The Christian shares the nature of God. Consequently, the world does not understand believers. The world never understood Jesus for who he was, the unique Son of God. "The reason why the world does not know us is that it did not know him" (3:1). The point is that if the world did not recognize the supernaturalness of God's Son when he was incarnate, we should not be surprised that it does not recognize us. The world's hostility to believers is rooted in rejection of the Lord and his way. Jesus' way of life was the godly life, and even the best people stood condemned. The world prefers its own ideas and ways, and it rejects Jesus and his followers.

A Letter from the Father (2:28 to 3:3)

Becoming a child of God leads to a new kind of person but not a completion on earth. There is a "not yet" for each believer. "Beloved, we are God's children now; it does not yet appear what we shall be, but we know that when he appears we shall be like him, for we shall see him as he is" (3:2). The "now" serves a double purpose. It underlines the believers' change of character. It also introduces a contrast between the believers' present with the glorious future. The glory of the new birth on earth does not exhaust believers' relationship with God. We wait expectantly for what we shall be.

John admitted that he did not know the exact state and condition of the future. However, he did know that "we shall be like him." When the Lord returns, we shall become like Jesus. Of course, now we are like Jesus in that we are children of God, live in the light, and are free from sin. John did not state explicitly how we shall be like Jesus. More than likely, John was thinking about the completion of a process begun at conversion. Since the day of our conversion, God has been trying to make us into the image of his Son (cf. Rom. 8:9). John seemed to indicate that this process will be complete when the believer goes to heaven.

God's children are in process. The status of a new person comes with conversion. The reality of the new person unfolds as a child grows, develops, matures. The goal of growth is maturity in the likeness of Christ himself. Believers will realize ultimately what they were in the process of becoming. They will be complete in divine fellowship and Christlikeness.

The Challenge for God's Children: 1 John 3:3

In John's letters, he presented many truths for God's children. In our study of 1 John 2:28 to 3:2, we have noted a word of assurance to bewildered believers. They were upset by impostors, and John wanted God's children to have confidence. Then we noted some insights which God gave about the origin of Christian character. It comes because of a spiritual relationship with the Lord.

Also, we noted that John talked with God's children about their future. They were in the process *then* of becoming Christlike but they were *not yet* complete.

Oftentimes letters include a word of challenge. My dad would often slip in such lines as "study hard," "get your rest," "come to see us." The beloved apostle John gave words of challenge to the believer. The fact of the Lord's return is a challenge to God's children. This glorious hope is an incentive for constant watchfulness. "And every one who thus hopes in him purifies himself as he is pure" (3:3). John had made it clear that it was "the last hour." He expected the Lord's return at any moment.

The first-century believers had no idea that the Lord would delay his coming for at least eighteen hundred more years. They expected the imminent return of Christ. This is not to say that they were mistaken, but it is to say that every successive Christian generation should expect the Lord's final return at any time. Speculating that the Lord would wait eighteen hundred years or more would have produced apathy and maybe even immorality. Once I heard R. G. Lee, the famed Southern Baptist pastor and evangelist, say: "I believe that Jesus will come in my lifetime—before I die I shall see the Lord." When I first heard the statement, I did not think that he should make such a predictive statement. But the more I studied the New Testament the more I realized that this is the biblical position. Each Christian in each successive generation should anticipate the Lord's return in his or her lifetime. The hope mentioned in 3:2 will be an incentive to constant watchfulness of the Lord's return.

Expecting the Lord to return at any moment in our lifetime will also furnish an incentive for holy living. To have this hope will mean that we shall "purify ourselves." The word translated "purifieth" (v. 3, KJV) denotes the putting away of all that defiles us. The Septuagint, the Greek translation of the Old Testament, used "purifieth" for the high priest's purification before entering the holy of holies. In this reference, the word refers to moral and spiritual cleansing. The fact of knowing that Jesus is coming for his children

A Letter from the Father (2:28 to 3:3)

challenges each child to holy living. This incentive is more than just an exhortation. To "purify" ourselves will mean that we shall continue the process of becoming more like God in purity of character. To become like God will mean that we shall become what we were created to be.

Purity does not come instantaneously. The verb "purify" is in the present tense and means that believers keep on purifying themselves. Moral purity is not achieved by one decision or one ecstatic experience. It begins, of course, with a union with Christ. But purity comes as a result of constant communion with the Lord. The full possibilities inherent in a relationship to God as his children lasts throughout the days of our lives on earth. To know that we can become more like God and actualize what we are supposed to be presents quite a challenge.

Without a doubt 1 John reads like a letter from a father. It has tender expressions, "little children." It has authoritative demands. It has blessed assurances for terrified children. It has instructions for God's children to learn. It has strong challenges. First John is, indeed, a letter from the Father. Now what should we do with letters from our earthly fathers? Of course we read them carefully. They have credibility. They deserve our attention. They must be heeded. We are God's children. We have 1 John as a letter from the Heavenly Father. What will we do with this letter?

9
Let Me Show You My Children
1 John 3:4-18

Most parents take delight in showing their children to other people. This begins as soon as the baby is born. As new parents, my wife and I wanted our parents, our relatives, our friends, and even total strangers to see each newborn son. The practice of showing our sons has continued. Through their successive stages, we have taken pride in their physical, mental, and spiritual growth. At various accomplishments, such as kindergarten graduation, Little League baseball games, baptisms, basketball games, and choir programs, we have rejoiced that others could see our children. More than likely the process of showing off your children never ends.

Once I visited an elderly couple. A prominent part of their conversation was talk about their children. They took time to show me pictures of their daughter and their three sons. With each picture, the couple gave me interesting information. The daughter is married to a surgeon in Houston, Texas. The oldest son is a major in the Air Force; the middle son is a chemical engineer in a Western state; and the youngest son is a psychology professor in a North Carolina university. Then the couple told me about the daughter's husband and the wife of each son. Then, of course, they had to tell me about the grandchildren. The couple took great delight in showing me pictures of their grandchildren and telling me about them.

The apostle John took delight in the children of God. He had been with many of them when they united their lives with the Lord and experienced the new birth. The apostle had observed their spiritual growth. He had observed the accomplishments for the Lord's work. Some people had been claiming to be God's children, but they denied either the humanity or divinity of Jesus. These people even practiced deeds not typical of God's children. What a tragedy to have people to masquerade as children of God.

John gave insights into the authentic children of God (3:4-18). Perhaps the pivotal statement of the entire section is in verse 10. "By this it may be seen who are the children of God, and who are the children of the devil: whoever does not do right is not of God, nor he who does not love his brother."

An attempt to masquerade as another parent's son once occurred. A young man went to several churches across America claiming to be the son of a deceased seminary professor. The real son of the professor had a beautiful voice, and he used it for a ministry in the churches. The impostor convinced several churches that he was the professor's son, and some churches allowed him to sing in the worship services. His performances were pathetic. He could not match the singing talent of the real son.

Many people masquerade as children of God in today's world. They try to convince people that they are God's children. Yet, as time passes, the impostors demonstrate that they do not belong to God's family. Their characters do not coincide with the Father's nature. They have none of the loving actions of the Father. Because these people are not in union and communion with the Lord, they are no match for God's children. Let us study carefully 1 John 3:4-18 so that we may see the characteristics of God's children.

A High Standard: 1 John 3:4-6

Generally speaking, parents have various expectations for their children. Some parents may expect too much from their children. They look for perfect report cards, outstanding athletic achievement, beauty queens, and absolute obedience. Other parents may expect too little. They show little concern for goals their children achieve.

John wrote about God's expectation for his children. God's goal for his children is always absolute, moral perfection. The Lord expects 100 percent commitment. He never reduced or compensated

Let Me Show You My Children (3:4-18)

for less than total commitment. The Lord never says, "You have my permission to be good 90 percent of the time." No, the Lord demands perfection. The ultimate goal of perfection is where God seeks to bring his children. Just because a child has not arrived at God's ultimate perfection does not mean God rejects the child. No, God works to move his children from where they are to where he wants them to be.

Failing to reach God's standard is a universal problem. Listen to John: "Every one who commits sin is guilty of lawlessness; sin is lawlessness" (3:4). John's first concern was to establish the fact that everyone falls short of God's standard. Twice John used universal expressions, "every one who" in verse 4 and "no one who" in verse 5. The reality of rebellion against God applies to every person, not just a few. God has his absolute standard, and everyone falls short of this ideal. Only one, namely Jesus Christ, has come up to God's standard.

The universal problem of human beings is sin. John made clear what he meant by sin. "Sin is . . . lawlessness." The idea inherent in the word "lawlessness" is opposition to God. It seems to mean more than the breaking of laws. The stress falls on persons desiring to have their way. Having that selfish desire causes transgressions against the law of God. Sin, according to John, is doing what you want to do rather than what God wants you to do. Because we rebel against God, we violate his holy law. Therefore, John established the fact that everyone falls short of God's standards.

What does God choose to do about this universal human dilemma? Does he leave us to struggle alone? Or, does he get involved in helping us to reach his standard? The answer is obvious from the biblical record and especially a study of 1 John. God works to help with human failure. "You know that he appeared to take away sins, and in him there is no sin" (3:5). John called attention to the life and ministry of Jesus Christ. He mentioned two specific aspects of the Lord's ministry, his sinlessness and his redemptive work to remove sin. God's ultimate attempt to remedy the universal problem of sin was in the earthly ministry of Jesus. The word "manifested" (KJV) (*ephanerōthē*) refers to Christ's appearing in the flesh, and it includes all he did while on earth.

A prominent part of Jesus' ministry was "to take away sins." This expression means to lift or to carry, the notion of getting sin out of the life of a person. Jesus came in order to get sin out of the lives of his children. Notice that John used the plural "sins." The Lord wanted to take away every manifestation of his children's rebellion.

The removal of sin can be accomplished only by one who is qualified. Only Jesus has the qualifications. "In him there is no sin." In the essential nature of Jesus, sin did not dwell in his heart. Instead of rebelling against God, he obeyed the wishes of the Heavenly Father. Therefore, Jesus is qualified to help with removing rebellion and its results from our lives.

Having stated that human beings do not come up to God's standard and that the sinless Son of God works to remove our sins, John proceeded to give instructions on how to move toward God's standard. To move from where we are to where God wants us to be, we need to abide in the Lord. "No one who abides in him sins; no one who sins has either seen him or known him" (3:6). The key expression is "abides in him." It is the presiding metaphor throughout 1 John. It means to open life in union with the Lord, as well as to have a constant communion with the living Lord. Constant abiding in the Lord will be submission to one who is qualified and capable of moving us from where we are to where we ought to be. Since there is no sin in Jesus, it is obvious that if we abide in him we shall not sin either. So, the way to actualize God's standard is to abide in the Lord.

In John's discussion of how to actualize God's standard, he used some unusual expressions. For example, his statement "No one who abides in him sins" is a difficult one to interpret. Its difficulty is compounded by similar expressions: "He who commits sin is of the devil" (3:8) and "no one born of God commits sin" (3:9). Two main problems emerge as one reads these statements of

Let Me Show You My Children (3:4-18)

John. First, John had recognized the possibility of sin by believers in other places in the letter (cf. 1:6,8,10; 2:1). Second, our personal experiences will not coincide with these statements about sinlessness. How then do we interpret John's words about sinlessness? Let us look at several views:

1. Some say John was talking about a special group of believers. They had virtually achieved God's standard. However, nothing in the passage would lend itself to this kind of interpretation.
2. Others say John distinguished between deliberate and involuntary sins. According to this view, sinlessness occurred as a result of refusing sin deliberately. A close reading of John's letter will disclose no such division of sins.
3. A lot of interpreters of 1 John seek to explain these expressions with the tenses of the verbs. They stress that the verbs are in the present tense, and their explanation is that believers do not sin habitually. One may wonder whether such an important matter could rest solely on a grammatical subtlety.
4. Still another view is that the expressions depict the ideal character of God's children. The statement—"No one who abides in him sins"—depicts what the believer ought to be. The ideal standard for every child of God is sinlessness. To see a person sinning means one or two things. First, it could mean that this person has never opened his or her life to the Lord. There can be no abiding when there is no union. Not being united with the Lord means the inability to actualize God's potential. Second, it could mean that a person is united with the Lord, but he or she does not live in daily communion with the Lord.

John wanted his readers to look at what it means to be God's children. He started with the Father's intention for them, absolute perfection. No one except Jesus has reached God's standard, but God has made it possible to move in this direction. By abiding in the

Lord we can move to what God wants for our lives.

A Righteous Behavior: 1 John 3:7-10

John turned his thoughts from the believers' ideals to observation about their behavior. Verses 7-10 contain words which relate to behavior. The key word in these verses is "righteous." John looked first at the demonstration of behavior (v. 7-8). His conclusion was the one who does right belongs to God, and the one who lives a life of sin belongs to the devil. John then looked at the explanation of behavior (v. 9). Believers' behavior can only be attributed to God's work in their lives. John then called for an examination of behavior.

John's discussion of righteous behavior began with an insight about the demonstration of behavior. "Little children, let no one deceive you. He who does right is righteous, as he is righteous. He who commits sin is of the devil; for the devil has sinned from the beginning. The reason the Son of God appeared was to destroy the works of the devil" (3:7-8). God's children behave righteously out of being in relationship with God. Notice two words in verse 7, "does" and "is." According to John, righteous deeds proceeded from a person's being. Doing is the evidence of being. God's children demonstrate their inner being by what they do.

Likewise, the children of the devil demonstrate the essence of their being by their life-style. Look in verse 8 at the verbs, "commits" and "is." The action of sin comes from the essence of character. People who practice sin disclose themselves as children of the devil. Being of the devil means that self-centeredness is the ruling principle of life. The primary activity of the devil since the beginning of the human race has been to get people to live life selfishly rather than God's way.

The antithesis between the family of God and the family of the devil may be seen clearly. The children may be detected by their moral likeness to the kind of family. One who sins habitually demonstrates a likeness to the devil. The one who practices righteousness demonstrates a likeness to the Father. Behavior results

Let Me Show You My Children (3:4-18)

according to the essence of one's being. God takes pride in his children, for they act like him.

Closely akin to the demonstration of behavior is the explanation of behavior. John explained that character results from God's work in a person's life. "No one born of God commits sin; for God's nature abides in him, and he cannot sin because he is born of God" (3:9). The reason God's children practice righteousness is because of God's work in them. Two expressions help us understand God's work in an individual. The first expression is "born of God" (*gegennēmenos*) in verse 9. It is a metaphor used to describe a person who allowed God to perform an inward transformation. The thought is that a believer has a new relationship with God. This relationship leads to a new life. The point of the birth metaphor is that spiritual life comes from God's power.

The second expression is "God's nature" in verse 9. The implication of "God's nature" is that the new birth results in the acquisition of a new nature. The abiding presence of God's nature within a believer enables God's child to live a righteous life. To continue a life of sin would indicate that God's nature has never entered a person. The new birth and God's nature within a person help to explain the character of a child of God.

John used an unusual expression to describe the behavior of God's children. John said that God's child "cannot sin because he is born of God" (3:9). John seemed to depict what ought to be, namely a life free from sin. He gave the ideal. John was saying that people who abide in God cannot live consistently and deliberately contrary to God's nature, for God's nature abides in them.

After explaining the origin of character of God's children, John asked for observations. Look at people and determine what children belong to God by their behavior. "By this it may be seen who are the children of God, and who are the children of the devil: Whoever does not do right is not of God, nor he who does not love his brother" (3:10). As we look at people, two groups may be seen: the children of God and the children of the devil. One's parentage is either divine or diabolical. A person who does not behave in accordance with God's character is a child of the devil. A person who behaves in accordance with God's nature has opened life to God and lives out of that inward transformation of being. God takes delight in showing the world his children, for their behavior is like his.

A Noticeable Birthmark: 1 John 3:11-18

Having established that God's children have a high standard and a new nature, John proceeded to describe a noticeable distinctive of God's children. The believers' spiritual birthmark is a love for one another. Typical of his letter writing, John used no colors but black and white. He continued the stark contrast between the children of God and the children of the devil. The child of God has love as a birthmark, whereas the child of the devil has hatred as a birthmark.

The believer's birthmark of love comes with the birth from above or the spiritual birth. "For this is the message which you have heard from the beginning, that we should love one another" (3:11). The word "message" was John's summary word. He used it in 1:5 to describe the fundamental teaching concerning the character of God. In 3:11 John used the term to describe the fundamental trait of believers. "From the beginning" probably refers to the beginning of the readers' Christian lives. Since the initial moment of union with the Lord, love has been present. So, love belongs to the beginning of the Christian life.

The new birth and its birthmark give a sharp distinction between God's child and the child of the devil. John mentioned first those who have the characteristics of the evil one.

> For this is the message which you have heard from the beginning, that we should love one another, and not be like Cain who was of the evil one and murdered his brother. And why did he murder him? Because his own deeds were evil and his brother's righteous. Do not wonder, brethren, that the world hates you (3:11-13).

John made the contrast between believers and nonbelievers as

Let Me Show You My Children (3:4-18)

sharply and forcefully as possible by using the Old Testament story of Cain. John made Cain an example of nonbelievers. Cain was characterized by jealousy, hatred, and murder. Hatred and jealousy are the embryonic stages of murder.

John asked why Cain murdered Abel. Though his question was a reference to Cain, John probably thought of why believers are the objects of hatred from the world. John's answer to the question was simple. Cain, a wicked person, hated the goodness of his brother Abel. Nonbelievers hate the goodness of believers. Hatred is the world's response to the believers' righteous lives. This lack of love and the activity of hatred demonstrates that one either does not belong to God's family or has a serious fellowship problem with the Lord.

Having mentioned hatred as the characteristic of the children of the devil (v. 12-13), John proceeded to give love as the characteristic of the children of God (vv. 14-18). John turned from the world's hatred to the church's love. He wrote first about the evidence of love (vv. 14-15) and then about the essence of love (vv. 16-18).

Notice that the children of God give evidence of love. "We know that we have passed out of death into life, because we love the brethren. He who does not love abides in death. Any one who hated his brother is a murderer, and you know that no murderer has eternal life abiding in him" (vv. 14-15). The world has the characteristic of hate, but God's children do not hate. Love is John's surest test of being one of God's children. The lack of love is an evidence of spiritual death. Without a doubt, the birthmark of love cannot be hidden from God's children.

Having shown the evidence of love as a birthmark of believers, John proceeded to give the essence of love (vv. 16-18). The definition of love may be clearly seen in Jesus' life of self-sacrifice. "By this we know love, that he laid down his life for us; and we ought to lay down our lives for the brethren" (3:16). The meaning of love has been defined clearly in Jesus' ministry. Cain is the example of self-seeking, and Jesus is the supreme example of self-giving. Cain's hatred resulted in murder. Christ's love resulted in sacrifice for the sins of people. True love may be defined as the giving of self to another person.

Christ's love is not something only to be studied and admired. His love is to be copied. "We ought to lay down our lives for the brethren" (John 3:16). John knew that not every believer would die for others as Christ died. So, he spoke about another kind of self-giving. "But if any one has the world's goods and sees his brother in need, yet closes his heart against him, how does God's love abide in him?" (2:17). Frequent opportunities come to each believer to help a person in need. C. H. Dodd said that love is "the willingness to surrender that which has value for our own life, to enrich the life of another."[1] Believers bear the birthmark of a willingness to enrich the lives of needy people.

John closed his discussion of love with an exhortation. "Little children, let us not love in word or speech but in deed and in truth" (3:18). Love is not just feeling alone. It is a deed. Frederick B. Speakman, the famed pastor of Third Presbyterian Church in Pittsburgh, once wrote a book he called *Love Is Something You Do*. This title reflects John's sentiment exactly. True love is the birthmark of a believer, and it is expressed by loving actions to needy people.

John took a close look at God's children. He was delighted to be a part of this spiritual family. Taking a close look at God's family has helped us see the Heavenly Father's ideals for his children, the Heavenly Father's nature in his children, and the Father's love expressed through his children. Anyone can belong to this great family. There is no control of the new birth other than a person's unwillingness. To open life to Jesus Christ will admit a person into the family and a life of abiding in the Lord will make one think, look, and act like one of God's children.

10
Getting Help from God
1 John 3:19 to 4:6

Several decades ago an extremely optimistic attitude prevailed about the human race. The catch expression was "man has come of age." Perhaps no piece of literature represented this attitude more than Aldous Huxley's novel *Brave New World*. It was written in 1932, and the author imaginatively projected life on earth for the next one hundred years. Huxley's speculative projections of genetic engineering, massive industrialization, scientific technology, and glorified utilitarianism have almost become normal structures of reality in this half of the twentieth century. Huxley predicted a world where human beings would become more prominent, and God would become less a factor in human life.

Maybe in one sense the human race has come of age. Advanced education and technology enable us to handle numerous human problems. The human race has come a long way in learning about structuring human society, handling interpersonal problems, mastering the environment, knowing self, and improving living conditions. But one could raise serious questions about the assertion that the human race has outgrown its need for God. Oddly enough though, some humanistic writers think modern people ought to discard dependence upon God. Strange as it may sound, some "religious" writers deny the theology of childish dependence upon God. These secular and religious writers advocate that humanity has come of age. They mean the human race has learned to master its world so why seek help from God?

Looking at life about us would raise serious doubts about humanity's coming of age. In this half of the twentieth century automated, educated people are calling for help. Perhaps the musical rock group known as the Beatles represented the predicament of modern people as they played drums, electric guitars, and kept crying harmoniously, "Help! I need somebody." People are seeking help from psychologists, psychiatrists, ministers, and other counselors. In the city where I live, there is a twenty-four-hour telephone service called "The Crisis Line." According to their report, hundreds of calls come each week from people with problems ranging from contemplated suicide to mild depression. The cries for help raise serious questions about humanity come of age. Human beings exhaust human resources, and they have to turn to Someone beyond themselves.

Catherine Marshall, the wife of the famed Presbyterian minister Peter Marshall, wrote a book called *Beyond Ourselves*. As she reported about the various crises of her life, especially the death of her husband, she repeatedly said that help must be secured from the God who is beyond human resources.

Near the end of the first century, some well-meaning people who were interested in the Christian faith, sought to improve it. Because of their bent to intellectualism, they wanted to make Christianity intellectually respectable. These philosophers thought Christianity had come of age with secular philosophy and the intellectual thoughts of the times.

Believers in the Roman province of Asia were bewildered. The happiness of their Christian lives was disturbed. Should they continue to believe in the humanity of Jesus? Should they deny Jesus' divinity? Would it be possible to believe in both his humanity and his divinity? Could they have a spiritual experience with God and disregard his commands? These questions and numerous others sounded the alarm for help. The believers had difficulty understanding or explaining their faith. The Lord sent help to the disturbed disciples by means of the uniquely inspired letter of 1 John. It was a word from the Lord.

The believers asked many significant questions. What am I to

Getting Help from God (3:19 to 4:6)

believe? How do I have communion with the Lord? What teachers should I believe? Human reasoning could not answer these and other questions the believers posed. The apostle John gave them some help from beyond human reasoning. John discussed some crucial issues as help for a troubled heart, help for a close communion with the Lord, and help for a confused mind. Human reasoning has not taken us to the place yet where we can be immune to help from God.

Help for a Troubled Heart: 1 John 3:19-21

John wrote to people with troubled hearts. The fact that the believers were disturbed may be seen in such words as "reassure," "condemn," and "confidence." John did not state specifically what caused them to be disturbed. More than likely these false teachers helped to produce the trouble. The believers heard the intellectual reasonings of the false prophets. Doubts entered their minds about Jesus' character, as well as his commands.

The reality of a troubled heart is an inevitable experience. "By this we should know that we are of the truth, and reassure our hearts before him whenever our hearts condemn us" (3:19-20). The expression "whenever" was the writer's way of saying that believers at times have troubled hearts. For serenity to be disturbed is not unusual. Doubt appears periodically throughout the Christian pilgrimage.

Some of the greatest believers have gone through periods of doubt. Thomas, one of the Lord's apostles, doubted the reality of Christ's resurrection. Harry Emerson Fosdick, the former pastor of Riverside Church in New York, in his autobiography *The Living of These Days* told of doubts that hit him during his second year of college. Fosdick quit attending church services. Then he said that he began to doubt his doubts, and ultimately a radiant faith emerged. For fifty years Fosdick shared his faith with millions. Alfred Lord Tennyson said:

> There lives more faith in honest doubt,
> Believe me, than in half the creeds.

So, we should not be disturbed drastically if a period of doubt comes. "Whenever our hearts condemn us" means that doubt is an inevitable experience of the believer.

Knowing just what causes our doubts is often hard to determine. Maybe a general investigation into some causes of doubt would be helpful. Sometimes doubts arise from the accusations of other people. More than likely the false teachers in Asia made the believers feel unsure about their Christian standing and behavior. Doubts have come to me when other people, using their human reasonings, told me what I should do or what I should not do to be a Christian. In my teen years, I heard many people who said, "You can't be a Christian if you dance, smoke, cuss, attend movies, or play cards." Of course, this is just a representation of the prohibitions. Some of those same prohibitioners were commanders too. They said, "To be a Christian you must attend church, say your prayers, tithe your money, and do good deeds." The reasonings of others can cause us to doubt.

Dr. V. L. Stanfield, professor of preaching at New Orleans Baptist Theological Seminary, once spoke in a chapel service about the various approaches to the Christian life. He said that some would say, "Thou shalt not." Others would say, "Thou shalt." Frustration, unhappiness, and uncertainty arise from either one of those stances. Stanfield went on to say the Christian is not one who lives either by "Thou shalt not" or "Thou shalt." The Christian lives by "Thou." So, doubts come from those with prohibitions or with commands.

At other times, doubts may arise from an accusing conscience. John said that *our* hearts condemn *us*. *The New English Bible* renders "heart" as "conscience." Knowing God's absolute standards for us and knowing where we are in relationship to his standard could produce a condemning heart. Only Jesus has lived up to God's standard. If we are not careful, we could engage in painful self-condemnation. Doubts can come as a result of preoccupation with imperfection.

To know the fact and source of doubt is not enough. We need

help for our troubled hearts. "For God is greater than our hearts, and he knows everything. Beloved, if our hearts do not condemn us, we have confidence before God" (3:20-21). Help for a troubled heart comes neither from outside human beings nor from an inward conscience. Troubled hearts receive help from an omniscient, gracious God. The Lord knows all things, including our secret motives and deepest resolves, and he is more merciful to us than our accusers and our own consciences. God does not seek to condemn us but to give confidence to us.

Having a good conscience increases the believer's joy. "Beloved, if our hearts do not condemn us, we have confidence before God" (3:21). The word "confidence" (*parrēsian*) depicts the freedom of father and child in a good relationship. It depicts the attitude of one who has nothing to hide. In light of this verse, help for troubled hearts comes with a loving, growing relationship with the Lord. This fact alone is enough to help with our doubts.

Help for a Close Communion: 1 John 3:22-24

The false teachers in Asia bewildered the believers. These false teachers claimed to know the Lord and to be close to him, but they denied that he was the Son of God. Furthermore since their relationship was a "spiritual" relationship, they did not bother to obey Christ's commands. John wrote to help believers with the relationship and communion with the Lord.

Communion with the Lord begins with a union with him. "All who keep his commandments abide in him, and he in them. And by this we know that he abides in us, by the Spirit which he has given us" (3:24). Becoming a believer starts with allowing the Lord to abide or to take residency within us. No one has communion with the Lord who has not opened life to him. The Holy Spirit takes up residence and begins the process of giving Christlike qualities.

To open life to the Lord will mean an access to the Lord in prayer and a confidence in our praying. "And we receive from him whatever we ask, because we keep his commandments and do what pleases him" (3:22). One could easily take verse 22 out of context and say that prayer is a means of getting what we want. The verse needs to be read in the context of the paragraph. John had been talking about the relationship of a father to this child. No decent father would give a child a blank check for whatever he wanted. No, God answers our prayers because we, as his children, want to do whatever pleases God.

Being a child and having a father means much more than receiving gifts. It means a relationship. My father was more than one who disbursed cash, clothes, car keys, and other gifts. He helped bring me in the world. He was a companion to me. The greatest joy of my father was his presence, not his gifts. Likewise, communion with the Heavenly Father means more than getting gifts. It means a relationship. The more fully we enter into the relationship the more we shall ask in accordance with the Father's will.

Opening life to the Lord leads to an obedience to his commands. "And this is his commandment, that we should believe in the name of his Son Jesus Christ and love one another, just as he has commanded us. All who keep his commandments abide in him, and he in them" (3:23-24). The word "believe" (*pisteusōmen*) means "to unite or join life." Believing in Christ means that we allow God to unite his life with our lives. Some prominent things happen as a result of uniting life with the Lord. Obeying Christ's commands and loving one another are proofs that we believe. These proofs are not the conditions of the relationship with the Lord but the consequences.

The indwelling Holy Spirit assures the believers of a relationship and of fellowship with the Lord. "And by this we know that he abides in us, by the Spirit which he has given us" (3:24). The Holy Spirit inevitably manifests himself in our character. He empowers us to live righteous lives and to love one another. The unmistakable evidence of the Holy Spirit is Christlike character.

The believers in Asia did not need to listen to the false teachers. Opening life to the Lord started their relationship with the Lord. They did not need to doubt their closeness to God. They only needed

Getting Help from God (3:19 to 4:6)

to open more of their lives to the Lord. The more we open our lives the closer we are in communion with the Lord.

Help for a Confused Mind: 1 John 4:1-6

The believers in Asia were confused intellectually. Both the false prophets and the apostles claimed to be guided by the Spirit. The question arose, How could one determine who was inspired by God's Spirit? John gave a clarion call to test the spirits.

The need for a test was evident. "Beloved, do not believe every spirit but test the spirits to see whether they are of God; for many false prophets have gone out into the world" (4:1). What did John mean by these different spirits? Neil Alexander identified the false spirits with those mentioned in 2:19. These people had gone out of the church to spread their heresies. In John's day many voices clamored for attention, especially the Gnostics. There was the definite need for a test to determine the true and the false. The word "test" (*dokimazete*) means to prove the spirits. The word was often used to determine whether money was real or counterfeit. The believers needed to determine the real from the unreal.

In today's world, there are many ideas clamoring for our attention. Many cults are gaining in interest and support. Some of these groups claim special revelation to authenticate their particular doctrine. There is an urgent need for Christians to "test the spirits."

Moving from the need of a test, let us now look at the particular test to be used. "By this you know the Spirit of God: every spirit which confesses that Jesus Christ has come in the flesh is of God, and every spirit which does not confess Jesus is not of God. This is the spirit of antichrist, of which you heard that it was coming, and now it is in the world already" (4:2-3). "By this" (*en toutō*) is a pointer to the test itself. The one test of the true and false was a confession of the incarnation.

The Spirit of God makes two great acknowledgments. First, the Spirit confesses that Jesus is the Christ, the Messiah. To deny Jesus as the Messiah would leave Jesus as nothing more than a great religious prophet. Jesus was the Christ, the unique Lord of the kingdom of God. Second, the Spirit confesses that Jesus became a man. The Gnostics could never accept Jesus' incarnation. To deny that God came in the flesh would be to strike at the roots of the Christian faith. So, the test to apply to all the philosophies and ideas is, What place does Jesus have? Is he secondary or primary? Those who place Jesus as the preeminent Son of God can be trusted. The Holy Spirit glorified Jesus. Anyone who depreciates Jesus as God in the flesh cannot be trusted. They have failed the test.

God's people have deliverance from the dilemma of confusion. "Little children, you are of God, and have overcome them; for he who is in you is greater than he who is in the world" (4:4). Believers can rely on the inner resource of the Holy Spirit. He is stronger than the world. The evil spirit is great, but the Holy Spirit is greater. By the Spirit's illumination and power, we can be overcomers of the world and the evil one.

John concluded his idea about the confusion by distinguishing the false prophet from the true prophet. "They are of the world, therefore what they say is of the world, and the world listens to them. We are of God. Whoever knows God listens to us. By this we know the spirit of truth and the spirit of error" (4:5-6). The emphasis is on the personal pronouns "they" and "we." The word "they" refers to the world. The false prophets get both their message and their listeners from the world. The world listens to those who speak its language.

John used the personal pronoun "we" to refer to those who preached and practiced the apostolic message. The two expressions "*they* are of the world" and "*we* are of God" stand in striking contrast to each other. Whereas the false prophets belong to the world, the prophet with the Holy Spirit is one who derives his authority, message, and inspiration from God's Spirit. Also, there is a vital connection between message and hearers. The Holy Spirit who lives in believers gives discernment to recognize the Holy Spirit in the messenger.

So, believers do not need to be confused over the prevalence of many ideas. "By this we know the spirit of truth and the spirit of

Getting Help from God (3:19 to 4:6)

error" (4:6). We can test the different spirits and "know" (*ginōskomen*) the true one. The word translated "know" is a knowledge gained by experience. The true teachers have the Holy Spirit, and the hearers experience the Holy Spirit.

John's words were therapeutic. Believers needed help, and the apostle John gave them a word from God. Human reasoning would not suffice. Believers could only be helped with a word from God. God's people face many of the same dilemmas today. They have condemning hearts, problems about relationship with the Lord, and confused minds. The letter of 1 John is a word from the Lord. From 1 John, especially 1 John 3:19 to 4:6, we can get help from God.

11
Learning About a Loving God
1 John 4:7-12

G. A. Studdert-Kennedy, the English chaplain poet, told about an incident he had one night on the cliffs of Dover. He peered into the darkness across the English Channel. His mind was on what kind of force lingered in the darkness. As he thought about who may be in the darkness, his mind turned to the thoughts of who was behind the universe. He questioned, *Is there an Unseen Force that holds the world together? Is there really a God, and what does he feel about human beings?*

While pondering these questions, Studdert-Kennedy recalled the experience of a sentry on night duty during World War I. The sentry heard a sound in the darkness and asked, "Who goes there? Friend or Foe?" It was quite a relief when the sentry heard, "Friend!" On the cliffs of Dover, Studdert-Kennedy dared to ask the question to the Unseen Force in the darkness, "Who is out there, friend or foe?" The devout chaplain dared to believe that the answer was "Friend!"

False teachers in the Roman province had strange ideas about God. First-century Christians were bewildered over the nature and character of God. They were disturbed over what false teachers said about God. The Gnostics said that spirit was good and matter was evil. This premise distorted the apostolic assertions of God as Creator and of God becoming flesh. These prominent ideas of the false teachers caused the believers to ask, What kind of God is out there?

Throughout 1 John, the author was careful to give descriptions of God. John used three great declarations of God: "God is light"

(1:5), a statement about God's majesty and purity; "He [God] is righteous" (2:29), a statement about God's attributes and activity; God is love" (4:8), a statement about his quality of self-giving. The believers did not need to get their ideas about God from Gnostic, pagan philosophy. They could learn all they needed to know about God in the earthly life of Jesus.

Pagan ideas still prevail which distort the revelation of God in Jesus Christ. Some people picture God as a harsh judge, seeking to punish. To others God seems a gentle, doting parent. Some depict God as a capricious deity. Others conceive of the Lord as a provincial deity with special affinity for their kind of people. To some God is considered a legalist with plenty of rules for living. Some even think of God as a blob whom we cannot know and understand. Many in today's world are agnostic, and they are never comfortable in saying anything about God. Atheism, the denial of God's existence, has become popular. These concepts and many others bring serious questions about God. Is there really a God? If there is a God, is he a friend or a foe?

What can we do amid so many prevailing ideas about God? The best thing is to put human speculation aside and to take up the biblical revelation. In 1 John 4:7-12, we can learn a lot about God. With John's statement, "God is love," there is no reason to speculate who is out there, friend or foe. Let us study this section carefully and learn about a loving God.

Love, God's Preeminent Attribute: 1 John 4:7-8

John's discussion of God's nature and activity grew out of the expression "love one another." Three times, in verses 7-12, John used the expression: one, an earnest appeal (v. 7); another, an imperative duty (v. 11); and one, a visible evidence of the indwelling of God (v. 12). With the occurrence of each expression, John related the grounds for mutual love. The first motive for loving one another is based on God's attribute of love. God's nature is love. Because believers share his life, they can love one another.

John began his discussion about God with insights into love

Learning About a Loving God (4:7-12)

being God's preeminent attribute. Love has its origin and source in God. "Beloved, let us love one another; for love is of God. . . . He who does not love does not know God" (4:7-8). The expression "love is of God" is an interesting one. Literally, it could be translated "love proceeds out of God." It is God's nature to love. Just as a fire radiates heat and light, so it is God's nature to love.

Perhaps it would be helpful to understand the kind of love which radiates from God. In the Greek langauge there were three basic words for love: *philia, eros,* and *agapē. Philia* denoted affection of friendship between kindred spirits. The noun form was used only once in the New Testament (Jas. 4:4). The verbal form (*phileō*) is found more frequently. It was used to describe friendly relationships. *Eros* described the pleasure one derived from a person or object. This word does not appear in the New Testament. *Agapē* was the word used for God's kind of love. The word was practically coined by the New Testament writers. William Barclay described *agapē* as the kind of love which is not just an emotion which rises unbidden in our hearts, but a principle by which we deliberately live. It has to do with the will. It is a principle of the mind which decides to seek the highest good of a person.[1]

God's love differs from all other types of love. *Philia* may be used of a friendship. *Eros* may be used of a desire for sex, beauty, or truth. But God's kind of love differs drastically from all other types. Neil Alexander distinguished the three words: *eros* is all take, *philia* is give and take, *agapē* is all give.[2] Only God has pure, self-giving love. It has its origin with God.

In addition to love having its origin with God, love also is an integral part of God's existence. "For God is love" (4:8). To assert that God is love is to say that love is of the very essence of God. It is his preeminent attribute. C. H. Dodd pointed out that the statement "God is love" meant much more than an assertion that "God loves" or "God is loving." These latter phrases could mean that loving was only one of God's many commendable attributes or activities. No, the expression "God is love" implies that his predominant attribute is love, and all his activity is loving activity. If he creates, he creates in love. If he rules, he rules in love. If he judges, he judges in love. All that God does is the expression of his preeminent attribute which is to love.[3]

Many of the misconceptions about God could be avoided if the statement "God is love" is accepted. Whatever God does, even wrath and judgment, will be contained within his love. God is love through and through. He does not do anything which does not have the quality of love.

Love, God's Amazing Action: 1 John 4:9-10

John moved from a discussion of God's nature to speak of his historical action. There have been many manifestations of the love of God. Without a doubt, the inhabitants of heaven see God's love in action constantly. However, God's amazing action may be seen "among us." The love of God was undoubtedly seen in his choice and use of Israel. The primary manifestation of God's love was in the historical ministry of Jesus and in his sacrificial death. To understand more of God's love, we need to examine the life and ministry of Jesus.

The coming of Christ in human flesh is a concrete, historical revelation of God's love. "In this the love of God was made manifest among us, that God sent his only Son into the world, so that we might live through him" (4:9). The historical action of the incarnation was depicted with the expression "among us." That meant that Jesus could be seen, heard, and handled. The person of the incarnation was God's "only Son" (*monogenē*). It was the combination of two words which literally mean "to send from." Jesus was sent from the Father. To think of God sending his Son is an amazing action. Martin Luther, the sixteenth-century Reformer, once said: "If I were as our Lord God and these vile people were as disobedient as they now be, I would blow the world in pieces." That represents a human attitude, but that is not God's attitude. God loved the world so much that he gave his Son.

Not only is the incarnation a historical manifestation of God's love but so is the death of Christ. "In this is love, not that we loved

Learning About a Loving God (4:7-12)

God but that he loved us and sent his Son to be the expiation for our sins" (4:10). The incarnation is a great disclosure of God's love, but the atonement has to be an even greater manifestation of God's love. The Lord was not content just to send his Son, but he wanted to help human beings. The pagans measured the worth of an object before they attached affection. One loved the worthy people first, and the unworthy ones were not loved at all. God did not single out the people for whom Christ would die. He loved all, and he died for all.

The historical death of Jesus had a purpose. It was to be "the expiation for our sins." The word "expiation" (*hilasmon*) in the biblical usages conveys the idea of removing that which separates a person from God. When Jesus died for human beings, he was removing the alienation which existed between God and people. It was people who needed to be reconciled to God, not God to people. In the atonement, we get an insight into what God's love has done. He has made possible the forgiveness of sin.

There should be no doubt about God's specific, historical manifestations of love. Bethlehem and Golgotha prove his loving action. These two events in history tell us a lot about God. The God who was "out there" came "down here" to be our Friend and to die for us. Because of what he did for us, our imperative duty is to love one another.

Love, God's Continuing Activity: 1 John 4:11-12

John was not content to speak of love as an astounding attribute or an amazing historical action. He wanted his readers to know that God's love did not cease at the cross. John said that God's love is a continuing activity when believers love.

Loving one another is a tremendous possibility. "Beloved, if God so loved us, we also ought to love one another" (4:11). If loving as God loves were an impossibility, John would not have given the obligation to love one another. The word "ought" (*opheilomen*) is emphatic. It means a moral obligation. Believers are bound to love one another. This obligation is based on a union with the Lord. To be united with the Lord means that God shares his life with us. If he shares his life, he will share his love. Because God lives within us, we have the possibility of loving one another.

The possibility of loving as God loves is no vague matter. Christians have a pattern which they can follow—"God so loved." The stress is on "so" (*houtōs*). That means the kind of love God has, the believer is to have. It is a self-giving love.

Loving one another gives visualization to God's personhood. "No man has ever seen God; if we love one another, God abides in us" (4:12). If no one has seen God, how can he be known? In the Gospel of John, the writer said that God could be known by Jesus. "No one has ever seen God, the only Son, who is in the bosom of the Father, he has made him known" (John 1:18). John gave another way the Father's personhood could be visualized. When God's people love one another, others can see God in action. Loving one another is a sure sign that God has united his life with a person.

Many seek rationalistic evidences for the existence of God. Using various arguments, such as the ontological, cosmological, telelogical, and moral arguments, some seek to prove there is someone out there. These arguments have their place, but to many, they fall short of what was hoped from them. There seems to be one undeniable demonstration of God in today's world. It is when love takes place. Without love, all the talk about God becomes meaningless.

Loving one another also actualized God's purpose. "His love is perfected in us" (4:12). What is God's purpose? Simply stated, God wants human beings to live together in harmony. When people allow self-giving love to be expressed, God's purpose will be fulfilled. God's love finds appropriate expression in a believer's life. Love becomes concrete and visible by people loving one another.

In 1962 Ernest Gordon wrote a stimulating book which he called *Through the Valley of the Kwai*. It is a story of God's love in action. During World War II, Ernest Gordon spent three and one-half years in a Japanese prison camp. Gordon related many of the experiences. He told of how the prisoners first turned to God, expecting him to come to their aid immediately. As time passed and

Learning About a Loving God (4:7-12)

the prisoners were not delivered, they felt God had forsaken them. The Japanese soldiers treated the prisoners brutally. A selfish type of existence emerged among the prisoners. They fought with each other over the slightest provocation. They stole from each other. They refused to care for the sick and dying or even to bury their dead.

Gordon related how a miracle of love happened in the camp. It started when just a few people started practicing self-giving love. The prisoners nursed Ernest Gordon while he was seriously ill. One man starved to death while sharing food to keep another man alive. One prisoner took an undeserved execution rather than the entire work crew be executed. The self-giving love of the few became contagious. Prisoners began to help each other. They nursed the sick, helped the weak, comforted the dying, and buried the dead. The prisoners not only helped their fellow prisoners but they also found opportunities to help their enemies. Gordon wrote: "Selfishness, hatred, jealousy, greed were all anti-life. Love, self-sacrifice, mercy, and creative faith . . . were the essence of life, turning mere existence into living in its truest sense. These were the gifts of God to men."[4] Without a doubt this demonstrated God's love in action.

There is no need to be confused about who is "out there." No pagan ideas should distort the biblical portrait of God. John, in only six verses, gave us valuable insights about a loving God. We have seen that love is God's primary trait. Love is God's *modus operandi*. This attribute of love has been shown in the historical life and death of Jesus. God's love is clearly seen as believers practice love for one another. The Christ who came "down here" has shown and continues to show the nature and activity of the One who is "out there."

12
Making Sure You Are a Christian
1 John 4:13 to 5:5

Asking a simple question can often plague a person into serious doubt. Once I asked my wife a question, and she was thrown into a time of serious uncertainty. We had left in a hurry for Sunday School. After arriving at our classroom, I leaned over to my wife and asked, "Judy, did you turn off the stove?" I was not questioning my wife's efficiency. I was only wanting to make sure the stove was off. After remaining still a moment, with a puzzled look on her face, my wife whispered to me, "I'm going home to check on the stove." One question casually asked caused her to doubt.

False teachers in Asia caused unsettled feeling in the churches. They raised questions about Christian doctrine and morality which produced serious doubts. John mentioned the false teachers: "I write this to you about those who would deceive you" (2:26). Again, John said, "Little children, let no one deceive you" (3:7). John described the disturbers with three terms; "false prophets" (4:1) indicating that they were spokesmen for false teaching; "deceivers" (1 John 2:26; 3:7; 2 John 7) because they were leading people astray; and "antichrists" (2:18) because they denied the divine-human person of Jesus. Once these heretics had been in the church, but they had left to spread their pernicious lies. John R. W. Stott conjectured that their secession was due probably to their failure to convert many of the church members.[1]

The heretics raised questions of a doctrinal and an ethical nature. They asked believers: Was Jesus really human? Do you believe Jesus was really the Son of God? Do you really have to take

Christ's commands seriously? These questions and others like them left believers in a wavering, insecure state. Nothing robs believers' joy any more than doubts about the Christian gospel or their experience with the Lord.

John wrote to give assurance to bewildered believers. Perhaps there is no greater section in the Bible on Christian certainty than 1 John and especially 1 John 4:13 to 5:5. Notice the various times John assured: "By this we know" (v. 4:13), "so we know" (v. 4:16). "that we may have confidence" (v. 4:17), "by this we know" (5:2).

Questions arise periodically within believers which cause doubts. Rationalism produces doubt. Skepticism encourages doubt. Agnosticism causes one not to be sure. Moral permissiveness raises many questions. Science and technology want observable answers. One of our greatest needs is to make sure periodically of our Christian standing. John gave five characteristics which believers may use to make sure they are Christians.

Possessing the Holy Spirit: 1 John 4:13

A key word upon which John grounded Christian assurance was the word "abide" (*menō*). He used the word twenty-four times throughout the letter. Peter Rhea Jones said that the presiding metaphor of 1 John is that of "abiding in God."[2] To abide in the Lord denotes that God abides in the believer, and the believer abides with the Lord. No one can be sure of a relationship unless they are abiding in the Lord. This metaphor of abiding meant that one is inhabited by God's Holy Spirit.

The habitation of the Holy Spirit has a definite beginning. "By this we know that we abide in him and he in us, because he has given us of his Spirit" (4:13). When did God give us his Spirit? According to the New Testament, God gives his Spirit immediately when a person believes. According to George Curtiss in his book *Principles of Greek Etymology* the verb "believe" comes from a root word which means "to unite life." When a person allows God to enter, he comes within the person's life to abide or to take up residency. So,

Making Sure You Are a Christian (4:13 to 5:5)

when a person "faiths" God, the Holy Spirit takes up residence within the believer.

This new relationship has amazing results. The indwelling Spirit produces Christlike character in believers' lives. The moment we open our lives to the Lord, the Spirit begins the process of changing. During the Christian pilgrimage believers take on the Christlike qualities of love, joy, peace, kindness, goodness, faithfulness, gentleness, and self-control. God will produce what the believer will allow. The presence of these Christlike qualities brings assurance that the Holy Spirit is working.

The possession of the Holy Spirit brings inward assurance. The Spirit's witness assures our hearts. "And by this we know that he abides in us, by the Spirit which he has given us" (3:24). Paul said, "You have received the spirit of sonship. When we cry, 'Abba! Father!' it is the Spirit himself bearing witness with our Spirit that we are children of God" (Rom. 8:15-16). If we want to make sure that we are Christian, we must look for evidence of the Holy Spirit's working, and we must listen for his inward witness.

Confessing Jesus as the Son of God: 1 John 4:14-16

In addition to the possession of the Holy Spirit, John gave a further characteristic of a Christian. A real Christian is one who confesses Jesus as the Son of God. Assurance of a relationship with God cannot rest on ideas outside or contradictory to the historical fact of the gospel and to a person's involvement with it.

John started building groundwork for assurance by giving a summary of the gospel. "And we have seen and testify that the Father has sent his Son as the Savior of the world" (4:14). John wanted his readers to know the reality of the gospel. His knowledge of the gospel was based on firsthand, experiential information. He had been an eyewitness to Jesus, and he testified of the fact.

After giving his personal witness to the gospel, John went on to the facts of the gospel. Simply stated, the gospel is "that the Father has sent his Son as the Savior of the world." The world needed to be rescued from the domination of the evil one. The Father wanted to save the world, so he sent his Son to be the Savior. These are the basic facts of the gospel. We cannot get assurance from any other story.

John wanted to give more than a summary of the gospel. He gave the believer's involvement with the gospel. "Whoever confesses that Jesus is the Son of God, God abides in him, and he in God" (4:15). To appropriate the gospel one has to confess Christ as the Son of God.

Involvement with the gospel results in a life of love. "So we know and believe the love God has for us. God is love, and he who abides in love abides in God, and God abides in him" (4:16). A vital union with the Lord makes possible a life of love. Love is the fruit or evidence of confessing Jesus as the Son of God.

Believers need a point of reference to have assurance. Nothing brings more blessed assurance than to know that you have confessed Jesus as the Son of God. Nothing confirms this confession any more than the evidence of the indwelling Spirit. Being united with the Lord leads naturally to another characteristic of a true Christian.

Growing in the Love of God: 1 John 4:17-21

John had alluded repeatedly to the fact of God dwelling in the believer. The thought of the indwelling God was prominent in verses 13-16. John turned to an inevitable result of abiding in the Lord. It is to grow progressively in the love of God. "In this is love perfected with us" (4:17). The word "perfected" (*teteleiōtai*) means a growing experience. It means the development toward the mark of maturity. The believer's love is not flawless. It has to be developed.

A growing love leads to boldness on the day of judgment. "In this is love perfected with us, that we may have confidence for the day of judgment, because as he is so are we in this world" (4:17). As a result of God's abiding in us and our abiding in God, believers have confidence for the day of judgment. The word "confidence" (*parrēsian*) had been used two other times (2:28; 3:21), and in each

Making Sure You Are a Christian (4:13 to 5:5)

case it meant a freedom of speech. It means a fearless freedom. "The day of judgment" evidently was a reference to the end of the age when all people should give account of themselves to God.

Boldness is possible for believers on judgment day because "as he is so are we in the world." The reference in this expression is to our standing with God. In this world, our standing before God is the same as the glorified Lord. Jesus is God's beloved Son in whom he is well pleased. Believers, too, are God's children, and we can be assured that he has accepted us.

John's positive truth about boldness is stated negatively. "There is no fear in love, but perfect love casts out fear. For fear has to do with punishment, and he who fears is not perfected in love" (4:18). Fear is the opposite attitude of confidence. It means a dread. Love and fear are mutually exclusive. We cannot love God and hide from him in fear at the same time. Believers know God is a loving Father, and there is no fear in this type of relationship.

In the early teen years of my life, I had a dread of God. Perhaps this anxiety grew from a distorted image of God. Being a Christian, I knew that I shouldn't fear God. By studying the Bible and by daily communion with the Lord, I discovered God's real character. It was a blessed assurance for me to have confidence not dread in coming before God. Growing in love will lead to confidence even for "the day of judgment."

A growing love will also lead to benevolence during the days of our lives. "We love, because he first loved us. If any one says, 'I love God,' and hates his brother, he is a liar; for he who does not love his brother whom he has seen, cannot love God whom he has not seen. And this commandment we have from him, that he who loves God should love his brother also" (4:19-21). Another result of a growing love is love for human beings. For someone to claim to love God while hating human beings means you listen to a liar. Only loving action proves the truth of our profession. Professing to love an unseen God is an easy matter. This profession needs the proof of practicing benevolence toward other people. No one is flawless in loving others, but assurance comes when we see that we are growing in our concern for other people.

Making sure you are a Christian depends on your love. One sure evidence of a believer is a growing love for God. It is the love which dispels dread of God and builds a boldness to him. This love of God leads naturally to a love for others. So, to make sure you are a Christian ask yourself, *Do I love God and am I loving other people?*

Obeying the Lord's Commands: 1 John 5:1-3

John moved naturally to a fourth distinctive characteristic of a Christian: the trait of obeying the Lord's commands. Union with the Lord leads to an obedience. An experience with the Lord is not just a feeling of rapture or a formal acknowledgment. It is an involvement in obeying his commands.

"Every one who believes that Jesus is the Christ is a child of God, and every one who loves the parent loves the child" (5:1). John wanted his readers to know that obeying Christ grew out of a union and communion with the living Lord rather than observing legalistic rules. Two words depict the relationship: "believes" (*pisteuōn*) and "child of God" (*gegennētai*). To believe is to open our lives so that the Lord can join his life with us. When we believe, the Lord makes believers children of God. He puts us into the family of God. The term "child of God" is the same term used to describe the new birth. In other places in the Revised Standard Version, the word is translated "born" (2:29; 3:9). The new birth brings believers into a loving relationship with the Heavenly Father and his other children. Because of the relationship with the Father, the child obeys.

My wife and I occasionally leave notes for our two sons about chores to do after school. We might have four or five activities they need to do, such as rake the leaves, clean out the storage room, wash the car, or clean their rooms. These commands would be useless to other parents' sons. They would not obey them, for there is no relationship. Because our sons belong to our family, they obey the rules. It makes a difference when there is a relationship.

Making Sure You Are a Christian (4:13 to 5:5)

Closely akin to relationship producing obedience is obedience showing the reality of the relationship. "By this we know that we love the children of God, when we love God and obey his commandments" (5:2). When children obey their parents' wishes and commands, the obedience demonstrates the reality of a relationship. Loving the Lord and other members of God's family gives positive proof that one is a child of God. The greatest evidence that one could ever have for being a child of God would be to love God and keep his commandments.

Believers should not find obedience to the Lord's commands difficult. "For this is the love of God, that we keep his commandments. And his commandments are not burdensome" (5:3). Relationship with the Lord changes attitudes. The word "burdensome" (*bareiai*) literally means "heavy." It does not mean that the Lord's commands are effortlessly simple to fulfill. Rather, they are not irksome or burdensome. Why? Because the believer wants to fulfill the wishes of the Heavenly Father, the Creator and Redeemer.

An old story illustrates the truth of burdensome commands. A man saw a small boy carrying a larger boy on his back. The man asked, "Son, isn't that boy heavy?" The smaller boy replied, "No sir, he's not heavy, he's my brother!" So, Christians can say of Christ's command: "They are not heavy or burdensome. They are what our Lord wants us to do." Besides, the commands are for our good.

Our checking to make sure we are Christians continues. Now we ask, *Do I have a relationship with the Lord?* Have I opened my life to Him? If I have, do I desire to do what he wishes? Am I obeying Christ's commands? Do I find a joy in doing what the Lord wants? Assurance of salvation results from a vital union with the Lord which leads to obeying him.

Overcoming the World System: 1 John 5:4-5

John gave still another characteristic of a real Christian, ability to be an overcomer. The expression "overcomes the world" appears three times in verses 4 and 5. This suggests that the believer battles daily with an evil world system. This system consistently seeks to make us forget God and forsake his ways. Believers, though, do not have to be defeated by the world. They can be overcomers.

Victory over the world system originates out of a relationship with God. "For whatever is born of God overcomes the world" (5:4). Perhaps the idea of a relationship with God seems redundant. Yet, John spoke of love, obedience, righteousness, victory, and other attainments out of a relationship with the Lord. If it were not for the new life which comes from God and which is implanted within the believers, no victory would be possible with those who have experienced the divine faith. He who is within the Christian is greater then than he who is in the world. When a relationship is established with the Lord, victory is possible.

Just to have victory the moment we become Christians is not enough. The Christian life involves a daily battle with a world system, and this means that for us to have victory there must be a continuous exercise of faith. "And this is the victory that overcomes the world, our faith" (5:4). The Greek text seems to have a play on words which cannot be easily produced in an English version. Moffatt's translation helps us: "the conquest which conquers the world." The verb "overcomes" could have been a reference to several matters: Christ's victory at the cross, the believer's victory at conversion, or to the various occasions throughout the believer's life. I think John was referring to the victories over the world system which believers had experienced. The Christians in Asia Minor had won many battles with the world's moral, intellectual, and physical pressures. There were many more battles to come, but victory could come the same way, namely through appropriating faith.

John made clear that the means of the Christians' daily victory over an evil world system is faith. The general thought is that our faith is the means of appropriating God's power. It is the spiritual weapon by which the assaults of the world system are met and overcome. The Christians' first victory came with faith and future victories will come by faith.

Believers can celebrate victory over a world system. John

Making Sure You Are a Christian (4:13 to 5:5)

offered a victory statement and victory assertion. It reminds me of cheerleaders asking about a football team, "Who is number one?" The crowd responds, "We're number one!" "Who is it that overcomes the world but he who believes that Jesus is the Son of God?" (5:5). The pull of paganism is powerful with its godless world order, its false standards, its bad disposition, and its evil inclinations. Who can overcome such a power? Of course, the victors are believers with continuous faith. The battle is too great for any human being. The victorious faith of the Christian is trust in God as he is revealed in his Son, Jesus Christ. E. M. Blaiklock entitled his work on 1 John, *Faith Is the Victory*. He pointed out the assurance that the believers can overcome the world by their faith in Jesus. The hymnwriter, John H. Yates, celebrated victory:

> Faith is the victory! Faith is the victory!
> Oh, glorious victory That overcomes the world.

Questions will come to Christians from many directions in today's world. There is no reason to fear inquiry. We have 1 John to help us make sure we are Christians.

One night my wife and I were getting ready for bed. Just as I put my head on the pillow, she asked, "Are all the doors locked?"

I said, "Yes," for I wanted to go to sleep. But sleep would not come. Her question made me doubt if the doors were locked. I got out of bed and checked all three doors. They were locked. I went back to bed and slept. Nothing enhanced my rest more than making sure that the doors were locked. Questions will come about our standing with the Lord. Using 1 John 4:13 to 5:5, we can make sure of our relationship with the Lord.

13
Hearing from the Witnesses
1 John 5:6-12

Courtroom drama holds a strange fascination. Periodically, some court proceedings attract national or world attention. Several years ago many Americans became intrigued over the trial of Dr. Sam Shepherd, the prominent Ohio physician accused of the murder of his wife. Newspapers, magazines, radio, and television reported daily proceedings of the trial. Each witness heightened the suspense. The jury convicted Sam Shepherd, and the judge sentenced him to life in prison.

Several decades ago one of the most famous trials in American history took place in Dayton, Tennessee. John T. Scopes, a science teacher was indicted by the state of Tennessee for teaching evolution in high school classes. The Scopes trial lasted from July 10 to 21 of 1925. Scopes was represented by Clarence Darrow, the foremost criminal lawyer of the day. The prosecution was represented by William Jennings Bryan, the famous American politican and orator. Witnesses for and against evolution were brought to the stand. The case ended with a victory for the prosecution.

Soon after World War II the world was intrigued with the trial of Nazi officers. Many were accused of helping murder six million Jews. One movie entitled *Judgment at Nuremberg* dealt exclusively with the trial of German officers. The movie's star won an Academy Award, but even more significant was the amazing interest of the people in the proceedings of the war crimes trials.

What is it about these transactions in the courtroom that holds such great fascination? Perhaps the interest comes from the suspense of prosecutors trying to prove guilt and from defendents attempting to establish innocence. Both sides seek to convince a jury with their witnesses. In most cases, the fate of the defendant or defendants hangs on the credibility of the witnesses. A jury will hear the witnesses and return a verdict. Hearing the witnesses is an all-important part of the trial procedure.

Near the end of the first century in the Roman province of Asia, various testimonies circulated about the person of Jesus. People were making a decision based on these testimonies. On one hand, pagan ideas challenging both the humanity and divinity of Jesus of Nazareth were circulating.

On the other hand, the apostles and others proclaimed the uniqueness of Jesus. They asserted boldly that Jesus was God in the flesh. They affirmed the reality of his humanity and his divinity. People in Asia were thoroughly confused. John proceeded in his letter to give witness to the messiahship and divine sonship of Jesus. In twelve verses, John used the word *marturia* (translated "testimony" and "witness"), six times as a noun and four times in a verbal form. Without a doubt, John wanted people to hear the witnesses about Jesus. These witnesses dealt directly with the heretical doctrines of the false teachers. John presented the witnesses. It was, and is, up to the readers to decide about Jesus based on the witnesses' credibility and testimonies.

Cerinthianism and Docetism are not doctrines which circulate today with those names. Yet similar testimonies circulate about Jesus. Some deny that a man named Jesus ever lived. Serious-minded people say that Jesus was a figment of the imagination of Gospel writers. Bertrand Russell, the philosopher, said that he regarded the issue of whether Jesus ever lived an open question. Others may affirm the historicity of Jesus, but they deny his divine uniqueness. The publication of the book *The Myth of God Incarnate* (1977) edited by John Hick is representative of the widespread skepticism about the divinity of Jesus. However, many evangelical churches continue to affirm the reality of the historical Jesus, the unique Son of God. What is one to believe with these various reports?

Hearing from the Witnesses (5:6-12)

Believers in every generation need to hear the witnesses about Jesus. John spoke about people who believed that the human Jesus is the Christ or Son of God. Their faith rested on well-established grounds. These witnesses are trustworthy. Let us hear them.

The Historical Witness: 1 John 5:6

John turned first to the historical witness. He stressed the historical groundings of the Christian faith and assured his readers that the Christian gospel was a historical reality. It did not belong in the realm of a fantastic myth, fabricated by the apostles.

John began with an identity of the historic person. "This is he who came by water and blood, Jesus Christ" (5:6). John did not want his readers to miss some great truths about Jesus. The historical person of Jesus was one and the same with the eternal Son of God. We cannot help but notice the title which John gave to the Savior—"Jesus Christ." In 1 John "Jesus" was a reference to the human title of Jesus. The term "Christ" was a reference to the divine Son of God.

John also wanted to identify Jesus Christ with a recordable historical event. "This is he who came" (*ho elthon*). The Greek construction makes the "coming" refer to a definite historical event. The aorist participle indicated a past historical appearance. Jesus was born at Bethlehem, reared in Nazareth, and spent his earthly ministry all throughout Palestine. He was real! He is no figment of human imagination. He came to earth, and historians recorded the event. Josephus, the Jewish historian and general, wrote in his *Antiquities of the Jews* (AD 93) about the historicity of Jesus. Even Roman writers such as Pliny and Tacitus made reference to the historical Jesus. The readers of 1 John could have had access to two or more of the Gospel narratives. These literary pieces were unequaled testimonies to the historical Jesus. John identified Jesus as the eternal Son of God and the One who made his appearance on earth. "This is he."

After identifying the historical person, John proceeded to characterize Jesus' earthly ministry. "This is he who came by water and blood, Jesus Christ, not with water only but with the blood" (5:6). The divine Christ came in Jesus, and his coming was significantly characterized by two historical events, namely his baptism and death. Alfred Plummer said "This is the most perplexing passage in the New Testament."[1] Various interpretations of water and blood have been given:

1. The baptism refers to the ordinance of baptism, and the blood refers to the ordinance of the Lord's Supper. John Calvin and other Reformers took this view. The difficulty of taking the water and blood as ordinances is with the appropriate symbols. Water does signify baptism, but blood does not signify the Lord's Supper. It is symbolic of only one of the elements.
2. Some link the passage with the spear thrust into the side of Jesus, from which blood and water flowed (John 19:34-35). In 1 John we are told that Christ came "by" or "through" water and blood. At the crucifixion the blood and water came "out of him."
3. Water and blood represent historical experiences through which Jesus passed and witnessed in some sense to his divine-human person. Therefore, water has been taken as a reference to Jesus' baptism and blood to his death.

Unfortunately we do not know the word symbols which John used about water and blood. More than likely his original readers immediately knew the meaning. We can speculate about the meaning of the expression in the Ephesian church. The false teachers distinguished between Jesus and the Christ. According to theories held by some, Jesus was united with Christ at his baptism but became separated again before the cross. Therefore, to refute this notion John described the historical ministry with one who "came [through] water and blood." John stressed that the one who came from heaven passed through water and blood. The water and blood were references to actual events of the baptism and crucifixion of Jesus. John bent the language of the false teachers to his own incarnational theology. The Son of God really did become a man, performed a ministry, and died for us. God really and truly lived on earth and suffered for human beings. The first witness has testified. It was a testimony to the historical life and ministry of Jesus Christ.

The Divine Witness: 1 John 5:7-9

John and the other apostles could testify to the truths about the historical Jesus. They could report the significant events of his ministry, but behind their testimony was a greater testimony. This was the divine witness of the Holy Spirit. Jesus had promised his followers the witness of the Spirit: "But when the Counselor comes, whom I shall send to you from the Father, even the Spirit of truth, who proceeds from the Father, he will bear witness to me" (John 15:26). The Holy Spirit confirms the reality of the gospel to which believers have committed themselves.

The Holy Spirit gives a true testimony. "And the Spirit is the witness, because the Spirit is the truth" (5:7). The Revised Standard Version omits part of verse 7 which is in the King James Version. The King James Version reads, "For there are three that bear record in heaven, the Father, the Word and the Holy Ghost; and these three are one." This part of the verse is properly omitted because it isn't supported by the most valid manuscripts.

Pursuing the textual problem of verse 7 would be an interesting academic exercise. However, let us not forget the truth that John wanted his readers to get: the Holy Spirit's testimony to Jesus Christ is a true testimony. The Holy Spirit testifies to the reality of Jesus. He is competent to do so, Jesus said, because he is the "Spirit of truth" (John 15:26; 16:13). Without a doubt, the Holy Spirit is qualified to testify, for he always tells the truth about Jesus.

Not only does the Holy Spirit give a true testimony, he also gives a unified testimony. "There are three witnesses, the Spirit, the water, and the blood; and these three agree" (5:8). The false teachers in John's day could not agree about Jesus. Human testimonies cannot agree about Jesus today. The divine witnesses—the Spirit, the water, and the blood—are in perfect agreement. John used three witnesses. According to the law in Bible times, no charge could be preferred against a person in court unless it could be confirmed by the evidence of two of three witnesses (Deut. 19:15).

The first of the three witnesses is the Holy Spirit. The Holy Spirit was active throughout Jesus' earthly ministry. When Jesus was baptized, the Holy Spirit descended in a special way (Mark 1:9-11). John the Baptist also said that Jesus would come to "baptize you with the Holy Spirit" (Mark 1:8). Jesus brought the Spirit to the people. The history of the New Testament church was continued proof that Jesus could give the Spirit to people. The full manifestation of the Holy Spirit came at Pentecost, and he repeated himself over and again in the history and experience of the church. Jesus possessed the Holy Spirit, and Jesus could give the Spirit. The continuing work of the Holy Spirit in the world and in the church is an undeniable witness to the reality of Jesus.

The second witness is the water. When Jesus was baptized, the Spirit descended on Jesus. Also, the Father said, "Thou art my beloved Son; with thee I am well pleased" (Mark 1:11). Water in this reference seems to refer to Christian baptism. When a person was baptized in the New Testament church, it was a symbol of a radical break with an old life. In Christ a person became a new creature. Christian baptism was a second witness to the continuing power of Jesus Christ.

The third witness is the blood. The death of Christ was the perfect sacrifice for sin. It reconciles people to God and gives them peace. The death of Christ is an experience within believers' lives which attests to the power of Jesus Christ.

The three witnesses—Spirit, water, and blood—have a united witness. These witnesses testify to the reality of Jesus' life. These witnesses also testify to the continued gift of the Spirit, the continued power of God to change lives, and the continued availability of Christ's atonement.

Having seen that the divine witness is true and unified, we see that God's witness is greater. "If we receive the testimony of men, the testimony of God is greater; for this is the testimony of God that he has born witness to his Son" (5:9). A triple human witness is enough to establish a fact. How much more should a triple divine witness be regarded as convincing! Divine testimony is much stronger than human testimony.

The Experiential Witness: 1 John 5:10-12

Two kinds of witnesses have testified. There have been historical and divine witnesses. Having heard from these outward witnesses, John proceeded to give the experiential witness. This was the testimony of a person who had experienced the transforming power of Jesus Christ. History yields facts about Jesus. The Holy Spirit testifies to truths about Jesus, but individual believers have the experience of inward transformation.

People have all kinds of "religious experiences," so we need to establish the kind of experience which John mentioned. John spoke of the "faith experience." "He who believes in the Son of God has the testimony in himself. He who does not believe God has made him a liar, because he has not believed in the testimony that God has borne to his Son" (5:10). The believer has the reality of Christ in his or her heart because of faith. The word "believes" (*pisteuōn*) means "to join life." When a person opens life to God, the Lord joins his life with the person. Therefore, the authentic experience with the Lord is when a person believes in the Lord. That is basic to assurance.

Many kinds of religious experiences are reported. In 1902 William James wrote a famous book called *The Varieties of Religious Experience*. The basic theme of the book is that people experience God in many ways. The one common denominator though in each genuine experience is to believe or to open life to God. To open one's life to God will mean that one has the "[witness] in himself." This means there is yet a deeper assurance.

The nonbeliever forfeits one of the greatest testimonies to Christianity. Refusing to believe means one refuses to experience the power of Christ. Failing to open one's life to the living Lord means that one considers God to be false. The nonbeliever does not have the witness of experience.

After discussing the kind of experience, John turned to the content of the testimony. "And this is the testimony, that God gave us eternal life, and this life is in his Son. He who has the Son has life; he who has not the Son of God has not life" (5:11-12). The essence of the Christian experience is "eternal life" (*aiōnion*). The word literally means "belonging to the age to come" or "God's kind of life." The word means much more than an endless existence. It means a qualitative life. The believer has the experience of God's kind of life.

Believers have excellent inward testimonies, for they have God's kind of life. This means many qualities. William Barclay enumerates five noticeable ones. In God there is peace; therefore, eternal life means serenity. In God there is power; therefore, eternal life means the defeat of frustration. In God there is holiness; therefore, eternal life means the defeat of sin. In God there is love; therefore, eternal life means the end of bitterness and hatred. In God there is life; therefore, eternal life means the defeat of death.[2] Only those who have opened life to God have this type of life. Those experiences bring amazing testimonies to the reality of Jesus.

John knew that many ideas circulated about Jesus Christ. He wanted to witness to the reality of Jesus and to an authentic Christianity. The key word in verses 6-10 is "witness" (*marturia* in the noun form and *martureō* in the verb form). Without a doubt, John wanted his readers to hear credible testimonies to Jesus Christ. Upon hearing these witnesses—the historical, the divine, the experiential—a person has to decide. Well, what is your verdict?

14
Making Gigantic Affirmations
1 John 5:13-21

J. B. Priestly, the British novelist, was asked by a magazine editor to write a short article on his religious beliefs. Priestly declined the invitation saying at the moment he was "perhaps better able to deny than to affirm." Then the novelist added wistfully, "I regret this, because now is the time for gigantic affirmations."[1]

In John's day, many people took the opportunity to deny many apostolic claims. Some interpretations of the faith by false teachers conveyed the impression that one didn't need either to believe much or to behave much to call oneself a practicing Christian. In fact, the less one believed, the false teachers asserted, the better. Also, these heretics said that one could be a professing Christian and live in the flesh as one pleased. What one did in one's spirit was what mattered to them, not what one did with one's body.

Toward the end of the first century these false teachers were seeking to get the church to discard many apostolic proclamations, such as belief in the humanity and deity of Jesus, the security of the believer, God's ability to keep, God's being available in prayer, obligation for self-giving love, obeying Christ's commands, moral purity, and other primary proclamations. Surprisingly, many of the false teachers had once belonged to the church, but they considered it "better able to deny than to affirm."

John wrote a letter to combat the heresies and to affirm some Christian certainties. Throughout the letter John took opportunities to give some "gigantic affirmations." The last verses are basically a recapitulation of the entire letter. A prominent theme throughout 1 John has been to increase the believers' joy, and John felt that the believers' happiness could be helped by affirming Christian certainties.

Even a casual reading of verses 13-21 will disclose the prominence of the word "know" (*oida* in six references and *ginōskō* in one reference 5:20*b*). These two words may be found at least forty times in 1 John (*ginōskō,* twenty-five times and *oida,* fifteen times). Generally speaking, *oida* means "to arrive at a steady, factual certainty," and *ginōskō* means "to know as a matter of experience." Perhaps no rigid distinction should be made in these words. John used *oida* prominently in the last verses to give some great Christian certainties. These certainties arose out of a relationship with the living Lord.

Christianity faces a crisis in today's world. The crisis is as great as any time in the course of history. Over the past one hundred years, some of the traditional certainties have been exposed to skepticism. Believers are compelled to face brash challenges to basic beliefs. Large numbers of people in both the East and the West are convinced that modern people have outgrown religion altogether. A new secularism has emerged which considers the Christian faith outdated and unintelligible. Many consider it liberating to discard concern for the ways of God. Some put their hopes totally on science. Others accept what they call the absurdities of life, and they exist in meaninglessness and despair. Without a doubt, our world needs to hear someone who can conscientiously give gigantic affirmations. Let us hear John's certainties about eternal life, prayer, character, and God.

An Assurance of Eternal Life: 1 John 5:13

John wrote to a church in which there had arisen divergent teachings regarding the nature of Christian belief. Such a situation made the members wonder if they possessed eternal life. The believers had been upset by the false teachers and become unsure of their spiritual state. Having declared to the readers that eternal life was to be found only in Jesus Christ, the Son of God (5:11-12), John proceeded to assure the believers. He wanted to strengthen believers

Making Gigantic Affirmations (5:13-21)

who might be tempted to doubt the reality of their Christian experience. Those who have opened their lives to Jesus Christ can be sure of their possession of eternal life.

John recognized that believers at times may doubt their Christian experience. "I write this to you who believe on the name of the Son of God, that you may know that you have eternal life" (5:13). Doubting our Christian experience can arise at anytime during the believer's earthly pilgrimage. There are times when the causes of doubt cannot be detected. However, the origin of doubt to the readers of 1 John is evident. It was caused by the false teachers. These false teachers who had seceded from the church presented rationalistic, intellectual arguments against some basic Christian affirmations. They raised serious questions to the believers, such as, Could the human carpenter from Nazareth really be the Son of God? or Could the eternal God come to earth and become a human being? Nothing raised doubts any more than the well-worded intellectual attacks. These intellectual presentations caused the believers to have to think through the reality of the Christian gospel and the validity of their Christian experience.

Serious-minded scholars in today's world question many traditional Christian affirmations. Is there really a God or is God a figment of human imagination? Did God really create the world or is the universe a result of evolution? Was there really a historical Jesus or was he the figment of Mark's mind? Is the historical Jesus really the Son of God, or was he just another great religious leader? Isn't one religion just as good as another, or do you have to believe in Jesus to be saved? These questions and numerous others presented to believers can cause serious doubt. To be a Christian one need not fear or evade intellectual investigation. Some of the greatest believers have been and are people who have gone through serious intellectual investigation.

Doubts arise not only from intellectual investigation but also from other sources. John did not mention these explicitly, but they are causes of uncertainty. Some believers go through periods of doubt because of the high standards of Christianity. Seeing what

God demands of us and knowing what we are could easily bring a doubting mind. Confidence can only come by acknowledging that we, as believers, take up the slack gradually from what we are to what we ought to be. Others have doubts because of feelings. I have heard people say, "I don't feel saved." Maybe the feeling of doubt arises out of intellectual investigations, God's high expectations, or other areas. Building a life on feeling can be a dangerous matter. Feelings change as often as the winds. At times, they change without predictability. To feel or not to feel one is a Christian should not be the basis for certainty.

What is the basis for certainty? How can we really be sure we are Christians? John said, "believe in the name of the Son of God." This means that we open our lives to Jesus, and the Lord joins his life with ours, the believers. Such a union leads inevitably to certainty about Jesus, to moral purity, and to love for one another. The question about grounds for assurance is, *Have I opened my life to Jesus Christ*?

Nothing increases the believers' joy any more than assurance. The hymnwriter, Fanny J. Crosby, caught the ecstacy of certainty when she exclaimed:

> Blessed assurance, Jesus is mine!
> Oh, what a foretaste of glory divine!

Believers can have assurance. There is no reason to linger in doubt. It is time for gigantic affirmation about the assurance of eternal life.

A Confidence in Prayer: 1 John 5:14-17

John moved to another gigantic Christian affirmation. This affirmation was that a believer could have confidence in prayer. The word which John used for "confidence" was *parrēsia,* "a boldness toward God." It conveys the idea of a child having the freedom of speaking to his father. To discuss the believers' confidence in prayer John spoke of two important elements of praying, namely petition and intercession.

Believers may offer petitions confidently. "And this is the

Making Gigantic Affirmations (5:13-21)

confidence which we have in him, that if we ask anything according to his will he hears us. And if we know that he hears us in whatever we ask, we know that we have obtained the requests made of him" (John 5:14-15). Knowing that we can petition God brings great confidence. Several helpful insights emerge from John's teaching about petitions. First, believers can be assured that God hears the petitions of his people. The eternal God attends to the wishes of his people. It is not just that our petitions register with God, but it is that God takes note of the petitions and listens carefully to them.

A second helpful insight we learn from John's teaching about petition is that requests must be asked according to God's will. Jesus taught us to pray, "Thy will be done." C. H. Dodd said, "Prayer rightly considered is not a device for employing the resources of omnipotence to fulfill our own desires, but a means by which our desires may be redirected according to the mind of God, and made into channels for the forces of His will."[2] True prayer is not asking God for what we want but asking him for what he wants.

A third insight about petitions is that God answers our requests. "We know that we have obtained the requests made of him" (5:15). We know that God hears us. We know that God answers our prayers according to his will. We also know experientially that God answers our prayers. The believers' prayers are not just words. Results happen when we pray. The believers may have confidence in the requests made to God.

Confidence in prayer comes not only in petition made to God but also in intercession to God on behalf of others. One of the hardest sections to interpret in 1 John is 5:16-17. John was writing to believers bewildered by seceders from the church. Every verse in 1 John needs to be interpreted in the light of that first-century situation. Other situations brought into these verses could be unfair. "If any one sees his brother committing what is not a mortal sin, he will ask, and God will give him life for those whose sin is not mortal. There is sin which is mortal; I do not say that one is to pray for that. All wrongdoing is sin, but there is sin which is not mortal" (5:16-17). In these verses, the stress is on intercessory prayer. John wanted people to pray for believers influenced by the false teachers. In John's view, there was little use in praying for those who actively denied the reality of Jesus.

The expression translated "mortal sin" in the Revised Standard Version is rendered "sin unto death" in the King James Version. The Greek expression is *pros thanaton,* and the literal meaning is "the sin which is going toward death." Apparently John's readers knew immediately the meaning of the phrase, but its meaning has been lost. Opinions vary with regard to John's usage of the expression. Several views are prominent:

(1) Some say it refers to a specific sin. Perhaps the genesis of this kind of thought went to the Old Testament distinction between capital offenses and those not capital offenses. Later in church history, sin was classified into categories of forgivable and unforgivable sins.

(2) Some say it refers to apostasy. These interpreters think John referred to people who once were believers but repudiated their faith. Other teachings of the Scriptures on the security of the believer seem to rule out this interpretation.

(3) Some say the expression refers to the blasphemy against the Holy Spirit. This sin, committed by the Pharisees, was a deliberate repudiation of known truth.

(4) Some say that the sin unto death refers to a physical death inflicted on a Christian by God as a result of a Christian's persisting in some sin. This would be akin to that which happened to Ananias and Sapphira (cf. Acts 5:1-11).

In light of the first-century life situation, the reference to "sin unto death" (KJV) (*pros thanaton*) speaks of two kinds of sinners. The first type of sinner is the one who sins against the will. This type of person hates his sin. Probably these are the people for whom John wanted his readers to pray. They had been influenced by false teachers, and they were not deliberately repudiating Jesus. These people needed the prayers of the Ephesian Christians. The second type of sinner is the one who sins willfully. More than likely these were the people who deliberately denounced the Lord. This is the kind of person who is going toward death. He or she has made sin a style of life. Sorrow or terror no longer fill his or her life. This person is on the way to a state where repentance is no longer possible. According to John's view, there was little need to engage in intercessory prayer for this kind of person.

Let us not lose sight of the gigantic affirmation. Basically speaking, in verses 14-17 John asserted a confidence in prayer. Believers could ask for needs in accordance with God's will, and their prayers would be heard. Believers could intercede for fellow Christians affected by the false teaching, and they would be helped. Glorious is the person who believes in the power of prayer.

A Victory in Jesus: 1 John 5:18-19

John continued with certainties. The expression "we know" is conspicuous in verses 18 and 19. This affirmation is that the believer has victory in Jesus Christ the Son of God. B. F. Wescott said *oida* in these usages expressed a state of certainty.[3] John declared what he and his fellow believers knew for a certainty: the assurance that Christians have victory over sin and an evil world system.

Believers can rejoice in being begotten of God. "We know that any one born of God does not sin" (5:18). The believer is described as one who has been born of God (*gegennēmenos*). In the Greek this is a perfect participle, and it would indicate that the new birth is an entrance into God's family with abiding results. God's children remain continuously in the family with amazing privileges and binding obligations. John mentioned one great obligation of God's child—"does not sin." This presents the ideal obligation which God gives to his children. If God gives this ideal standard, he will work with his children to bring them from where they are to where they ought to be.

Believers need not remain the way they are when they enter into God's family. Growth is possible. By opening life to the Lord, he will unite with the believer's life to give victory over self-centeredness. The believer can have victory over any sin he or she desires. Throughout the pilgrimage of the Christian life, selfish desires emerge. There is victory in Jesus Christ.

Christians are not only begotten by God but they are also kept by God. "He who was born of God keeps him, and the evil one does not touch him" (5:18). The subject of the verse is Christ. He is the one who changes a person. The thought is not the believer keeps himself, but that Christ keeps the believer. The word for "keeps" (*terei*) is a graphic one. It meant to watch over so as to preserve and protect. Why do believers need to be guarded? If we have been begotten of God, are we not free of sin? Of course not. The wicked one stays maliciously active in believers' lives. He seeks to get believers to live selfishly rather than in God's selfless way. The super strength and amazing subtlety could be more than a match for an individual believer. The Son of God came to destroy the works of the devil and to guard his children so that the devil cannot touch them. The word rendered "touch" (*haptetai*) means that the evil one cannot cling to believers. The evil one may wound at times, but he cannot inflict mortal blows to believers. Victory is possible over the evil one because of the presence of the Guardian.

Because believers are born into God's family there is a noticeable mark of ownership. Believers rejoice because they belong to God. "We know that we are of God, and the whole world is in the power of the evil one" (5:19). Nonbelievers are in the grasp of the evil one. Over against that dark picture, John gave the picture of the victorious believers. "We are of God." The lines are clearly drawn. Either we belong to Jesus, or we belong to the world. There is no third category for the undecided.

An Understanding of God: 1 John 5:20-21

The crowning certainty which John shared is that faith in Jesus enables the Christian to understand God. Three times in verse 20 John used the word "true" (*alethinos*). It refers to the genuine as opposed to the counterfeit. The false teachers did not have a certainty about God. They were unsure. Over against that uncertainty was the believers' certainty. The Christians did not guess about the nature of God. An understanding of God had been reached

Making Gigantic Affirmations (5:13-21)

by the historical Jesus. God was in Christ. The time of guessing about God was over. It was a time for gigantic affirmations about the true God.

How do believers arrive at this understanding of God? John gave two criteria for the discerning of the real God, namely historical manifestation and personal experience. "And we know that the Son of God has come and has given us understanding, to know him who is true; and we are in him who is true in the Son Jesus Christ" (5:20). The first criterion for understanding God is his historical manifestation in Jesus. "The Son of God has come." The verb could mean has come or is here. Once again John reminded his readers that the believers' faith is based on the historical fact of the incarnation and the abiding presence of Christ.

The second criterion for understanding God is personal experience. In the last part of verse 20, John used several words and expressions which described the believers' personal experience with the Lord; "understanding," "know," "in him," and "in his Son Jesus Christ." Any objective person could discover the facts of the incarnation, but the believer has an "understanding" (*dianoin*) of God. As a result of opening life to the Lord, the Christian has another facility for discerning the true God.

The second occurrence of "know" in verse 20 differs from the first occurrence. The second word is *ginōskōmen,* and it means a knowledge gained only by experience. The present tense verb would imply that the experiential knowledge is not just the one isolated event of conversion, but it is a continuous and progressive experience. Anyone can "know" (*oida*) the facts of the incarnation, but believers "know" (*ginsko*) the person of the incarnation.

The two expressions "in him" and "in his Son Jesus Christ" refer to the believers' union with the Lord. To be in Jesus is to know the Father. The true God, the creator, sustainer, redeemer of the universe, may be experienced by opening life to Jesus who came and is here.

After giving the criterion for understanding God, John made two bold statements about God. "This is the true God and eternal life" (5:20). The first statement is that the historical Jesus is a manifestation of the true God. We can get no greater insight about the true God than from Jesus. The sense of the statement could be paraphrased as follows: "This—the God about whom I have written in the letter, the God who is light and love, the God who has been disclosed to us by his Son, and with whom we live in vital union—is the real God." The second bold statement is that Jesus makes eternal life possible. The Gnostics taught that there were numerous ways to enter into God's life. However, John said eternal life was only through Jesus Christ.

John closed his letter with a warning against false gods. "Little children, keep yourselves from idols" (5:21). A. E. Brooks in his work on 1 John in *The International Critical Commentary* thinks that the allusion to idols was a reference to the untrue mental images fashioned by the false teachers. Their false view of the Son and of the Father created a heinous idolatry. John called believers to focus on the true God.

Near the end of the first century numerous ideas circulated about Jesus Christ. The believers were bewildered over these diverse views which were so different from the apostolic proclamation and their personal experience. What should they do? Should they just talk about Jesus as the Son of God, among fellow believers? Or should they rethink the incarnation or their experience? Or even worse should they deny Jesus? John helped them. He told them that it was a time of gigantic, positive affirmations about Jesus Christ.

What should be the Christians' word to our contemporary age? Should we "tone down" the incarnation? Should we be silent altogether? Or, is this a time better to deny than to affirm? No, this is an age where the time has come to proclaim the certainties of the Christian faith.

Notes

CHAPTER 1
1. Neil Alexander, *The Epistles of John* ("The Torch Bible Commentaries") New York: The Macmillan Company, 1928, pp. 32-39.
2. Peter Rhea Jones, "A Structural Analysis of I John" in *Review and Expositor*, Vol. LXVII, No. 4, pp. 439-440.
3. Ibid.

CHAPTER 2
1. Edward A. McDowell, "I, II, III John" (*The Broadman Bible Commentary*, Vol. 12) Nashville, Broadman Press, 1972, p. 195.
2. Alfred Plummer, *The Epistles of John* ("Thornapple Commentaries") Grand Rapids: Baker Book House, 1980.
3. John R. W. Stott, *The Epistles of John* ("The Tyndale New Testament Commentaries") London: The Tyndale Press, p. 58.

CHAPTER 5
1. Stott, pp. 96-97.

CHAPTER 6
1. C. H. Dodd, *The Johannine Epistles* ("The Moffatt New Testament Commentary") London: Hodder and Stoughton, 1966, p. 41.
2. William Barclay, *The Letters of John and Jude* ("The Daily Study Bible") Philadelphia: The Westminster Press, 1961, p. 68.
3. Dodd, p. 41.
4. Dodd, p. 42.

CHAPTER 7
1. Dodd, p. 53.
2. Dodd, pp. 53-54.

CHAPTER 9
1. Dodd, p. 86.

CHAPTER 11
1. Barclay, p. 115.
2. Alexander, p. 94.
3. Dodd, p. 110.
4. Ernest Gordon, *Through the Valley of the Kwai* (New York: Harper and Brothers, 1962), p. 109.

CHAPTER 12
1. Stott, p. 105.
2. Jones, p. 442.

CHAPTER 13
1. Plummer, p. 113.
2. Barclay, p. 134.

CHAPTER 14
1. A. Leonard Griffith, *Ephesians: A Positive Affirmation* (Waco, Texas: Word Books, 1975), p. 13.
2. Dodd, p. 134.
3. B. F. Westcott, Commentary On *The Epistles of Saint John* (Grand Rapids: William B. Eerdmans Publishing Company, 1966), p. 193.